P9-CEG-806

Daily Life of Early Christians

Daily Life of Early Christians

by

J. G. DAVIES

GREENWOOD PRESS, PUBLISHERS
NEW YORK

Reprinted by permission
of Meredith Press

First Greenwood Reprinting 1969

Library of Congress Catalogue Card Number 75-91757

SBN 8371-2413-1

PRINTED IN UNITED STATES OF AMERICA

Acknowledgments

I wish to express my thanks to the Reverend Canon S. L. Greenslade, Van Mildert Professor of Divinity in the University of Durham, for his incisive and helpful criticism of the whole book, and to Mr. G. Templeman, Lecturer in History in the University of Birmingham, for his assistance in developing my ideas on "The Nature and Scope of Church Social History" as set down in Appendix III.

J. G. D.

The University,
Birmingham, England

Introduction

I WISH that it were possible to meet with one who could deliver to us the history of the Apostles, not only all they wrote and spoke of, but of the rest of their daily life, even what they ate, and when they ate, when they walked, and where they sat, what they did every day, in what parts they were, into what house they entered, and where they lodged — to relate everything with minute exactness, so replete with advantage is all that was done by them . . . for when a man leads a spiritual life, the habit, the walk, the words and actions of such a one, in short all that relates to him, profits the hearers, and nothing is a hindrance or impediment.[1]

These words of John Chrysostom, Bishop of Constantinople, at the end of the fourth century, A.D., express, as clearly as any have done since, the purpose of social history, which is to depict the daily life of our ancestors in all its complexity.

The practices and customs of the early Christians, the pattern of their life as exemplifying their faith, is to

[1] Chrysostom, *In Philemon, exord.*

many quite unknown, for, although the social historian has presented a great number of vivid pictures of pagan society in the first centuries of our era, the Church historian has so far been slow to follow in his footsteps. And yet in the records of the primitive Church there is a wealth of information about the likes and dislikes, the habits and superstitions, the clothes and the food of its faithful and unfaithful members. It is true that there is a certain overlap between what we might term secular social history and Church social history, but at the same time there is a considerable difference between them.[2]

Like Israel of old, the New Israel, the Church, stood in sharp opposition, even antagonism, to the pagan culture which formed its environment; sacred and secular were clearly distinct, and since secular, at least under the Roman emperors before Constantine, meant pagan, Christians lived a life apart, aloof from their polytheistic and frequently immoral neighbors and all the paraphernalia of day-to-day living in a society dominated by emperor cults, mystery religions and the worship of an ever-expanding pantheon of gods. What sort of life did the early Christians lead in their isolation and how did the conversion of Constantine affect it? It is the purpose of these studies to attempt in part an answer to these questions.

[2] A more detailed analysis of this distinction is given in Appendix III, page 254.

We begin with Clement, a Christian philosopher and teacher in Alexandria at the end of the second century: a man who sought to make a bridge between his beliefs and those of the cultured class to which he belonged both by birth and education. Clement was acutely aware of the distinction between the Christian way of life and the pagan, but his missionary ardor, typical of many at that period, impelled him to observe and criticize all that he saw and to utilize pagan modes of thought for the propagation of the faith. He is representative of the many apologists who preceded him and a forerunner of the many intellectual giants who were equally zealous in the task of conversion. There were unfortunately others in the Church who showed equal zeal, but in wrongdoing — one such was Paul of Samosata, who in the mid-third century lived licentiously and taught heretically at Antioch: a man who, as his contemporaries expressed it, acted "as though he was not a bishop but a sophist and a charlatan." Here we see the reverse of the picture, a readiness to compromise with pagan ideas and pagan morals. To omit it would tend to falsification, presenting an idealized representation which falls short of the truth; to include it is to bring out by contrast the spiritual stature of those many Christians who, unlike Paul, refused to follow the easy road of capitulation to the world.

An interval of forty years brings us to Carthage in the midst of the bloodshed and horror of the Diocletian persecution, and to the martyr Victoria in particular. It may seem strange in a description of daily life to include an account of the last day in any individual's earthly existence, but, although the Church enjoyed long periods of peace in the first three hundred years and although persecution was often only spasmodic and shortlived, to become a Christian was to accept the possibility, if not the certainty, of ending one's life on the rack or in the amphitheater. Such a possibility profoundly affected the Christian's attitude to contemporary society, intensifying his hostility to it, and to omit any reference would be to pass over in silence an important feature of the life of the early Church as a whole.[3] By the middle of the fourth century, with the conversion of Constantine an event in the past, persecution was no longer an imminent reality; and in Rome Diogenes the sexton, who typifies the humble working-class Christian, could rejoice in the easing of the tension between the Church and the state, while experiencing a certain professional regret at the consequent abandonment of the catacombs in favor of open-air cemeteries. Fifty years later, John Chrysostom, one of the great bishops of the Church and occupier of the important see of Constantinople, had cause to lament the steady decay of the earlier social dualism; his biting strictures on contemporary society echo the satire

[3] The fact of martyrdom emphasizes more than anything else the refusal of the majority of Christians to compromise their absolute renunciation of the world.

of Clement, but what especially nauseated him was that the behavior and fashions he so deprecated were those of his own congregation; the world was crowding into the Church. It was a reaction to this acute secularization that the monastic movement began; the first monks fled not only from the world but from the world in the Church — in so doing they saved the Church and Christianity. Regarded at first with much suspicion by those in official quarters, the support of such men as Basil of Caesarea, Jerome, Augustine and John Chrysostom won for the monks a rightful place in the Church. Although the West was behind the East in its readiness to accept the movement, the work of John Cassian, our final character, himself a friend of Chrysostom, at Marseilles in the second and third decades of the fifth century, did much to allay hostility; and he indeed was the true father of Western monasticism; whether a Benedict of Nursia or a Benedict of Aniane or a Bernard set out to systematize or reform, it was upon his foundations that they built. So the present study ends with an account of the thought and ways of that individual who was to play such an important part in the medieval period — the monk.

The most radical omission in this brief series of studies is the portrait of a Christian lady — virgin, matron or widow — apart from the martyr Victoria. The reason for this is twofold: in the first place, the Christian woman lived a secluded life, seldom leaving the house except to go to church, carefully veiled when she did so in order not to see or to be seen by the lewd-eyed pagans she passed in the street. At home her tasks were simple and limited; she helped with the cooking, made clothes, and devoted herself to prayer and Bible reading. Happy and dignified though her daily life may have been, it was, while not humdrum, sufficiently unvaried to be incapable of sustained and detailed description.[4] In the second place, in the few instances where more details are forthcoming, they concern those ladies who practiced the ascetic life either at home, like Jerome's disciple Marcella in Rome, or in a nunnery, like Macrina, whose brother Gregory of Nyssa wrote her biography; but their daily life was little different from that of the monk of whom more vivid accounts have been preserved and who therefore appears in the present work in the person of John Cassian.

The extent to which imagination should play a part in this reconstruction is a delicate question to decide. How far, for example, is it legitimate to employ direct speech, which is so much more vivid than indirect?[5]

[4] Cf. J. Donaldson, *Woman, Her Position and Influence among the Early Christians,* 1907.

[5] Cf. Toynbee's reference to the method of Thucydides: "His *oratio recta,* while more vivid, is really no more fictional than the laboured *oratio obliqua* in which the moderns present their composite photographs of public opinion." (*The Study of History,* abridged ed., 1945, p. 45.)

The general principle, however, is easily discernible: no statement should be made, no description given, no remark reported, which is not based upon verifiable evidence. But to provide each fact with its appropriate reference to a contemporary document would be to overload the text, rendering it almost unreadable; instead, a list of authorities for each chapter is appended for those who would either check them or pursue the subject further. The list may be safely ignored by the general reader. For him, however, some footnotes have been printed where their substance is such as to be of interest either by adding to or by further explicating what has been said in the text.

One further problem remains, namely, the trustworthiness of the sources themselves and in particular, when sermons are used, how far precept reflects practice; a homily exhorting to the practice of a virtue is not sufficient evidence to conclude that the audience is addicted to the vice opposite to that virtue. A long and minute discussion of each statement would be tedious in the extreme; the general reader must obviously accept on trust what is here recorded, making use of the references if he so desires. But this much may be said, that where the writings of a Christian can be compared with those of a contemporary pagan there is a notable unanimity of observation (Libanius and Ammianus Marcellinus both provided independent testimony to the truth of Chrysostom's picture of his age);

and further, though there is something of a deterioration of Christian life, there is good reason to suppose that precept and practice were in closer agreement in this period than has often been the case in subsequent ages.

Contents

APPENDICES

Daily Life of Early Christians

1

Clement, A Philosopher of Alexandria

A.D. 200

CLEMENT of Alexandria or Titus Flavius Clemens, to give him his full name, was born of heathen parents, probably in Athens, about the year A.D. 150. After studying rhetoric and philosophy at the university, he was converted to Christianity; there followed a period of travel, during which he visited the southern part of Italy and more particularly the eastern Mediterranean, where he attached himself to two teachers, one of them being an Assyrian and the other, whom he met in Palestine, being a Hebrew. After further journeyings he came at last to Alexandria, where he met Pantaenus, the first great head of the catechetical school in which the Christian was instructed in the faith and the pagan inquirer received answers to his questions. Clement after being the pupil of Pantaenus later became his associate in the conduct and oversight of the school, and about A.D. 190, having been ordained a presbyter of the Church, he succeeded his master and held office until the outbreak of the perse-

cution under Septimus Severus in 202. He then withdrew to Cappadocia and was the guest of a former pupil, Alexander, who later became Bishop of Jerusalem. In 211 Clement was the bearer of a letter from Alexander to the Church at Antioch; four years later he was dead.

If little is known of the details of Clement's public life, his personal character is familiar from those of his writings that have been preserved. Apart from some fragments called Selections from the Prophets, *a sermon entitled* Who is the rich man that shall be saved? *and a portion of an address to the newly baptized, there are three extant treatises which form a trilogy. The first, the* Exhortation to the Greeks, *was intended to convert the reader to Christianity; the second,* The Pedagogue *or* Tutor, *to instruct in the Christian way of life; and the third, the* Stromata *or* Miscellanies, *to which Clement referred as his "carpetbag" or, as we might say, "scrapbook," was a collection of diffuse material describing the ideal of a complete Christian, perfect in all spiritual knowledge. In these works Clement reveals himself as a man of profound learning, calm and peaceful in character, grave yet cheerful, solemn but not without a sense of humor, charitable and frank. With his gaze firmly fixed upon his Redeemer, with prayer ever on his lips, he sought not so much to impart information to his students as to knit them closer to their Lord. He was no abstract thinker, divorced from life; his ardent desire to convert his hearers is expressed again and again, and his vivid description of their pagan environment, together with his careful regulation of the minutiae of everyday Christian living, re-creates the contemporary scene in all its original freshness.*

Alexandria, towards the end of the second Christian century, with its three quarters of a million inhabitants, its pride of place next to the imperial capital itself, its thriving commerce and its famous university, hums with ceaseless activity like Virgil's beehive. At its great docks cargoes of Egyptian linen, glass and papyrus, of Arabian frankincense and leopard skins, and all of the diverse luxuries carried in the one hundred and twenty-four merchantmen which arrive each year from the Indian seas, are shipped for transit to Italy. From beneath the lighthouse, one of the seven wonders of the world, the great fleet, led by the massive three-thousand-tonner *Iris*, annually sets sail for Puteoli with a third of the Roman corn supply aboard. Along the canals which ring the city other vessels head for the Nile by way of Lake Mareotis, freighted with glassware for the Chinese court and with clothes for the natives of Abyssinia. Manufacturers, sailors, eastern traders throng the broad streets: there is no need for anyone to be idle in Alexandria. If the life of commerce is not to one's liking, then the famous museum, founded by Ptolemy Soter, provides the means for the study of literature, mathematics, astronomy, natural history and anatomy. Though the majority of the citizens may rave about horse racing and the theater and are forever stirring up riots, never satisfied until they have seen blood flow, there is yet ample opportunity in the city where Philo, the Jewish philospher, strove to reconcile pagan and Hebrew thought and where Galen, the greatest physician of his age, completed his training, for a scholar to pursue his studies in peace and with advantage both to himself and to those who may come to hear him expound the results of his learning. It is therefore in a setting by no means uncongenial that Titus Flavius Clemens, a Christian philosopher, seeks to bring others along the same path which he has followed in his search for truth.

As the sun comes up over the *regio Judaeorum,* the Jewish quarter of Alexandria, Clement, a light sleeper, is already shaking up his bed. He dresses slowly and methodically, passing his head and right arm through the opening in his toga and throwing the loose end across his chest and over his left shoulder. With his hair clipped so that it does not hang into his eyes, his mustache cut round by a pair of cropping scissors, and his beard, which has never been disturbed by a razor, long and flowing, there is little to distinguish him from many of his more seriously minded fellow citizens, except perhaps the purity of his white clothes, cut a little short to avoid their sweeping the dirt like a broom, and the absence of any footwear. The same simplicity is affected by his wife[1] who, in striking contrast to the brilliantly colored Indian silk dresses and the gold-plated bejeweled sandals in which so many Alexandrian ladies display themselves, puts on a white woolen tunic and untrimmed shoes. She binds her hair simply along the neck with a plain pin, disdaining the tresses and braidings, the dyeings and the wigs, which, as her husband is wont to remark, tend to keep so many of her sex awake at night for fear lest in their sleep they might disarrange the fantastic creations which it has taken them most of the day to put in order. Her toilet is now complete, for, believing that a woman ought to be adorned within and not without, she has no chains, collars, rings or bracelets, nor, since she thinks the best decoration for the ears is true instruction, has she her lobes pierced in ugly fashion to allow the passage of earrings or eardrops.

She takes her place by her husband's side; together they look through the open window towards the rising sun, heads and hands lifted to the heavens, and Clement raises his voice in this hymn of praise:

> Hail, O light! For in us, buried in darkness, shut up in the shadow of death, light has shone forth from heaven, purer than the sun, sweeter than life here

[1] It is probable, although not certain, that Clement was married. See R. B. Tollinton, *Clement of Alexandria*, 1914, I, pp. 271 f.

below. That light is eternal life, and whatever partakes of it lives. But night fears the light, and, hiding itself in terror, gives place to the day of the Lord. Sleepless light is now over all, and the West has given credence to the East. For this was the end of Thy new creation.

Prayer follows, not demands for the necessities of life, for Clement is sure that God who knows all things supplies the good with whatever is for their benefit, even though they do not ask; instead he thanks God for the past, for the present, and for the future as already present through faith; he prays to live the allotted life in the flesh, as free from the flesh; to attend to the best things and flee from the worse; for relief in those things in which he has sinned and conversion to the acknowledgment of them.

Turning to his wife, Clement salutes her with a kiss, an action he carefully avoids in front of the servants, and goes out into the atrium, where he finds his son sitting on the edge of the rain-water tank in the center of the open court. The young Clement is a quiet, rather shy boy, and Clement with a twinkle in his eye says chaffingly to his wife: "This son of mine is always talking!" The happy flush which this remark brings to the young lad's face soon gives place to a look of eager attention as he sits on the stone bench at his father's side for his daily lesson in the Christian faith.

Today's subject is prayer and Clement is concerned to teach his son both what it is and how to practice it.

"Prayer," he says, in his even, measured tone, "prayer is simply talking to God, conversing with God. There is however no need to say our prayers aloud; our inward desires are voiceless prayers to God. What we have to do is to concentrate our whole spiritual nature within on expression by the mind, in undistracted turning towards God. When we do this, even though we are praying alone, we do it in the society of angels and we have the choir of saints standing with us."

Clement pauses and looks at his son with his shrewd eyes to see if he is taking it in, and then continues:

"As you know, some people have definite times for prayer, for example, the third, sixth and ninth hours — but the true Christian prays throughout his whole life, trying by prayer to have fellowship with God. He can do this because, as I said, prayer does not have to be vocal. In every place, therefore, but unobtrusively, we can pray. You have only to form the thought in the secret chamber of your soul and call on the Father, and He is near, at your very side."

It is a theme dear to Clement's heart and his words flow on uninterrupted by his thoughtful son, until the sound of someone at the front door reminds him that it is nearly time for his first lecture, and so the lesson comes to an end, after he has given his son a portion of Scripture to be learned by heart. Together they stand for prayer:

> Lord, for long we have desired to receive Thee; we have lived according to what Thou hast enjoined, transgressing none of Thy commandments. Wherefore also we claim the promises. And we pray for what is beneficial, since it is not requisite to ask of Thee what is most excellent. And we shall take everything for good; even though the exercises that meet us, which Thine arrangement brings to us for the discipline of our steadfastness, appear to be evil.

Clement is head of the famous Alexandrian catechetical school, which has come into existence, not as the result of a deliberate official act by the Church but in answer to a vital need for instructing the believer in the rudiments of his faith and for providing the pagan inquirer with an introduction to this new religion. The curriculum worked out by Clement is not so detailed nor so comprehensive as that which his successor, Origen, is to adopt. Origen will begin his syllabus with a series of introductory lectures on philosophy, following this with courses on logic and dialectic, on the natural sciences, in particularly geometry and astrology, finally crowning them all with addresses on ethics and theology. Clement, who is essentially missionary-minded and sees his vocation not so much as an educator in all the important branches of human learning as that of a guide to Christ, opens his lectures with an attack upon paganism, leading up to an attempt to convert his hearers to Christianity; this is succeeded by instruction in the Christian way of life, and the whole reaches its completion in a long and careful description of the ideal of a perfect Christian initiated into the deep things of spiritual knowledge. Side by side with this, he prepares candidates for baptism and for the benefit of the faithful expounds the Scriptures, commenting in particular on the writings of the Prophets. Clement's aim therefore is to exhort, then to train, then to teach; in his own words it is "to improve the soul and to train it up to a virtuous, not to an intellectual life," and so he classifies his lectures as hortatory, preceptive and persuasive.

His audience has by now assembled in the dining room (triclinium), which he uses as a lecture hall and, notes in hand, Clement goes to his seat on the little raised dais. As he opens his book, his eyes rove over his students, observing their looks, their attitudes, their mannerisms, all those little signs which reveal their inner character and tell him of their capabilities.[2] There is Alexander, a keen and concentrated listener, a man with powers of leadership and authority in his bearing, the kind of person to make a good bishop.[3] Next to him is Leonidas, passionate and intense, devoted heart and soul to the faith he has newly embraced: the martyr

2 "He who addresses those who are present before him, tests them by time, and judges by his judgment, and from the others distinguishes him who can hear; watching the words, the manners, the habits, the life, the motions, the attitudes, the looks, the voice." (*Strom.* I, i.)

3 He later became Bishop of Jerusalem.

type.[4] By his side is his son Origen, only sixteen years old, but already full of promise, an embryonic genius — and perhaps not so much of an embryo. Then there are some Jews; they have started early to arrive in time from the *regio Judaeorum*, an indication of their dissatisfaction with the faith of their fathers. For the rest, they all come from Greek families with many centuries of culture behind them. It is a pity that there are no native Egyptians present, but after all not many of them are intelligent, and "teaching a fool is gluing a potsherd, and sharpening to sense a hopeless blockhead is bringing earth to sensation." They sit, some on stools, some on the uncarpeted floor; a few have notebooks, wax-coated tablets, fastened together by rings, with a stud in the center of each leaf to prevent their pressing together and so obliterating the writing which is executed on them with an iron stylus. They wait in quiet expectation for Clement to begin.

This is the second lecture in his introductory course in which he is concerned both to show the inadequacy of Greek philosophy and at the same time to emphasize the partial truths it contains. Clement knows that many of his less cultured brethren have scant sympathy with his approach; with their great North African contemporary, Tertullian, they are ready to say:

"What indeed has Athens to do with Jerusalem? What concord is there between the academy and the

[4] He was martyred in the Severian persecution.

Church? What between heretics and Christians? Our instruction comes from the 'porch of Solomon,' who has himself taught that 'the Lord should be sought in simplicity of heart.' Away with all attempts to produce a mottled Christianity of Stoic, Platonic and dialectic composition! We want no curious disputation after possessing Christ Jesus."

But Clement, with his Athenian education, cannot share this attitude; his own experience has taught him that the way to bring a person to Christ is to speak to him in language that he can understand; those who attend the museum and listen to the lectures on Aristotle — or rather, since he has dropped out of favour and Neoplatonism is now the fashion, to lectures on Plato — would not be affected by an appeal couched in the idiom of the market place. They are educated men, they need an intelligent approach, they need a bridge across which they may pass into the fold and that bridge is conveniently to hand in Greek philosophy. Moreover Clement, while convinced that the way of truth is one, is large-minded enough to believe and proclaim that "into it, as a perennial river, streams flow from all sides." Clement's opening words command the ready attention of his students:

> In our previous lecture we have seen the inadequacy of Greek mythology, its absurdity, its immorality, its utter unworthiness to be a vehicle of divine truth. Its stories are not only unedifying, they are shameful and

indecent. A vast crowd of the same description swarms upon me, bringing in their train, like a nightmare, an absurd picture of strange demons, speaking of monstrous shapes in old wives' tales. Far, indeed, are we from allowing grown men to listen to such talk. Even to our own children, when they are crying their heart out, as the saying goes, we are not in the habit of telling fabulous stories to soothe them; for we shrink from fostering in the children the atheism proclaimed by these men, who, though wise in their own conceits, have no more knowledge of the truth than infants. Why, pray, do you infect life with idols, imagining winds, air, fire, earth, stocks, stones, iron, this world itself — to be gods? Why babble in high-flown language about the divinity of the wandering stars to those men who have become real wanderers through this much vaunted — I will not call it astronomy, but — astrology? It is the Lord of the winds, the Lord of the fire, the Maker of the Universe, He who gives light to the sun that I long for. I seek for God Himself, not for the works of God.

Clement pauses and scans his audience to gauge the effect of his words.

I seek for God Himself, not for the works of God [he repeats]; who, then, am I to take as my helper in my search? We do not, if you have no objection, wholly disown Plato. How then, Plato, must we trace our God? "It is," to quote a passage from the Timaeus, "a hard task to find the Father and Maker of this Universe, and when you have found Him it is impossible to declare

Him fully." Why, pray, in God's name, why? "Because," as Plato says in his letters, "He can in no way be described." Well done, Plato, you have hit the truth. But do not give up. Join me in the search for the good. For into all men without exception, especially into those who are occupied with intellectual pursuits, a certain divine effluence has been instilled, wherefore they admit, even though reluctantly, that God is One, that He is unbegotten and indestructible, and that somewhere on high in the outermost spaces of heaven, to use a phrase of Menander, in His own private watchtower, He truly exists forever.

> Tell me what nature must man ascribe to God?
> He seeth all; yet ne'er Himself is seen,

says Euripides.

Clement's quiet but audible delivery goes on. Though the substance of what he has to say has required much thought and effort in preparation, he strives to express it simply and directly, avoiding eloquence, content with indicating his meaning, without framing his language with artfulness and care, not composing paltry sentences like gewgaws. Driving home his points with apt quotations from the authors with whom those present are so familiar, he shows that Plato speaks of God as the King of all things, as the measure of all existence; even Antisthenes, the founder of the Cynic philosophical school and the opponent of Plato, bears witness to the one true God. Xenophon, the pupil of Socrates, a one-time army general and later author, is aware that God cannot be represented in human form like the divinities of Olympus; and Cleanthes, the Stoic, who spent his nights drawing water in order to have the wherewithal to devote his days to philosophical pursuits, proclaims the holiness, the justice, the righteousness and the love of the Supreme Being; while even the Pythagoreans believe in the unity of God.

> These sayings [Clement emphasizes] have been recorded by their authors through God's inspiration, and we have selected them. As a guide to the full knowledge of God they are sufficient for every man who is able, even in small measure, to investigate the truth.

Clement stops speaking for a moment and turns a page in his notebook, ready to expound an allied but slightly different theme:

> But we will not rest content with philosophy alone. Let poetry also approach — poetry which is occupied entirely with what is false — to bear witness now at last to truth, or rather to confess before God its deviation into fable. Let whichever poet wishes come forward first. Aratus, then, perceives that the power of God pervades all things:
>
> Wherefore, that all things fresh and firm may grow,
> To Him our vows both first and last shall rise:
> Hail, Father, wonder great, great aid to men.
>
> In the same spirit Hesiod of Ascra also dimly speaks of God:

For He is king and master over all;
No other God hath vied with Him in power.

It may be freely granted [Clement continues, after adducing further testimonies from the poets] that the Greeks received some glimmering from the divine Word, and gave utterance to a few scraps of truth. Thus they bear witness that the force of truth is not hidden. On the other hand they expose their own weakness, since they failed to reach the end. For by this time, I think, it has become evident to you all that those who do anything or speak anything without the word of truth are like men struggling to walk without feet.

The lecture is ended and Clement rises.

Let us pray. Be gracious, O Teacher, to us Thy children, Father, Charioteer of Israel, Son and Father, both in One, O Lord. Grant to us who obey Thy precepts, that we may perfect the likeness of the image, and with all our power know Him who is the good God and not a harsh judge. And do Thou Thyself cause that all of us who have our conversation in Thy peace, who have been translated into Thy commonwealth, having sailed tranquilly over the billows of sin, may be wafted in calm by Thy Holy Spirit, by the ineffable wisdom, by night and day to the perfect day; and giving thanks may praise, and praising thank the Alone Father and Son, Son and Father, the Son, Instructor and Teacher, with the Holy Spirit, all in One, in whom is all, for whom all is One, for whom is eternity, whose members we all are, whose glory the celestial spirits and angels are; for the All-good, All-lovely, All-wise, All-just one. To whom be glory both now and forever. Amen.

As he makes his way out into the atrium, Clement is stopped by one of his audience, anxious for him to answer a question.

"Sir," he says, with a slight twitching of the corners of the mouth, suggesting that he is not entirely serious in his inquiry, "sir, although this is not immediately apposite to what you have been saying today, I should be glad if you would resolve a difficulty for me. I understand," he continues, as Clement signifies his attention with a courtly inclination of the head, "that your Master said, 'He that looketh on a woman to lust after her, hath committed adultery.' Now surely when He said this, He did not mean to condemn the mere desire, but the going beyond the desire and the action which results from so doing? Perhaps you will allow me to illustrate my point with a story? A young man once fell in love with a courtesan and persuaded the girl, for an agreed sum, to come to him on the following day. But, his desire being unexpectedly satisfied, by laying hold of the girl in a dream by anticipation, when the girl came as arranged he refused to see her. But when she heard what had happened, she demanded payment on the grounds that she was the cause of his desire being satisfied. The matter eventually came to court, and the judge ordered the youth to hold up the purse containing the money in the sun, and then told the courtesan to take hold of the shadow, facetiously bidding him pay the image of a reward for the image of an embrace."

"When one dreams," replies Clement, somewhat shortly, for he doubts the sincerity of the questioner, "the soul assents to the vision. But you dream while awake whenever you look on someone to lust after her; not only, as you say, if along with the sight of the woman you imagine intercourse with her in your mind, for this is already the act of lust, as lust; but if one looks on beauty of person and the flesh seems to you in the way of lust to be fair, regarding carnally and sinfully, you are judged because you admire. On the other hand, he who in chaste love looks on beauty thinks not that the flesh is beautiful, but the spirit, admiring, it seems to me, the body as an image, by whose beauty he transports himself up to the Artist and to the true beauty."

With a polite bow Clement dismisses the inquirer, and as he turns away his wife appears from the kitchen.

"A mouse has been gnawing the bag of flour," she complains in an exasperated tone.

He, with a smile at her worried look, replies:

"There's nothing surprising, my dear, in a mouse gnawing a bag; but it would have been a matter for concern if the bag had been gnawing the mouse!"

Her laughter relieves her feelings and she returns to

the kitchen, while Clement goes to talk with the poor beggar [5] on whose account his wife is engaged in baking bread.[6] He has not much time to spare before his next lecture, but sufficient to stem his guest's profuse thanks by saying that he regards himself only as the steward of such material goods as he possesses and therefore happy to dispense them to those in need. The two say the Lord's Prayer together and then Clement, re-entering the triclinium, takes his seat on the dais once more.

His audience this time consists entirely of believers, of those who only a few days ago have come to the end of their period of probation, their catechumenate, and have been made members of the Church. The memory of the simple but impressive ceremonial is still fresh in their minds. As night was falling on Easter Eve they had gone to the house which through the generosity of a wealthy member of the congregation had been placed at the disposal of the Church as a place of worship.[7] Entering from the street through a

[5] There are frequent references in Clement's writings to the Christian's duties to the poor, for example, *Strom.* II, xix, VII, xii. The importance of almsgiving was stressed in numerous tracts, such as Cyprian, *De opere et eleemos.* Even the heathen were impressed by their generous charity. See Julian, *Ep. xlix Ad Arsac.*

[6] There is no need to describe the baking, for methods have changed little; an interesting account, based on extensive discoveries, is given by T. H. Dyer, *Pompeii,* 1868, pp. 353–360.

[7] Although there is no archaeological evidence of separate church buildings at this period, from literary allusions it is apparent that they were in existence. See *Chronicle of Arbela;* Tertullian, *De spect.,* xxv; *De pudic.,* iv; *De idol.,* vii. At the same time the local congrega-

door on the right into the baptistery, a long narrow room with the font surmounted by a canopy on pillars at one end. Soon the bishop and his presbyters, of whom Clement is one, had made their entrance, and the water was consecrated by invoking the Name of God. They, the candidates, had then come forward to make their renunciation of the devil and all his pomp, following this by a profession of faith as they recited the creed in answer to questions put to them by one of the presbyters. The Baptism itself had followed, each candidate stepping forward separately and bending over the font; water was poured over his head three times while the presbyter uttered the threefold formula: "I baptize thee in the Name of the Father, of the Son, and the Holy Spirit."[8] Dressed in white robes, representing their newborn innocence, they had then knelt before the bishop, who had anointed them and laid his hands upon them, "invoking and inviting

tions in each area continued to meet for worship in private houses. It is impossible to say what was the situation in Alexandria in Clement's day as his references are ambiguous (cf. *Strom.*, VII, v), but it is assumed that a house-church was in existence. The description in the text is based upon that of the Christian house-church, *c.* A.D. 232, discovered at Dura-Europos on the Euphrates. See M. Rostovtzeff, *Dura-Europos and Its Art*, 1938, pp. 130–134.

[8] Most writers on the subject of Christian initiation assume that immersion was the early practice. This is in flat contradiction to the archaeological data to which C. F. Rogers called attention in his *Baptism and Christian Archaeology* (*Studia Biblica et ecclesiastica*, V, pt. iv), 1903. Other more recent evidence entirely supports his conclusion that affusion was the normal custom. See J. Lassus, *Sanctuaires chrétiens de Syrie*, 1947. Certainly the Dura font, described in the text, excluded immersion.

the Holy Spirit through the words of benediction."[9] Then, incorporated into the Body of Christ, adopted into God's family, they had tasted milk and honey, symbolizing the first fruits of the promised land. Crossing the courtyard, they had taken their place in the room on the opposite side where the Church gathered for worship and, as Easter Day dawned, the Eucharist had begun.[10]

Clement himself was responsible for preparing them for this great occasion and to him is allotted the further task of continuing their instruction in the faith. Today he does not want to enter into profound theological arguments or to expound the intricacies of philosophy; instead he wishes to tell these neophytes something of the ideal of Christian conduct as he understands it. Looking round to satisfy himself that all the newly baptized are present, he begins, dispensing with any verbose introduction.[11]

> Practice quietness in word, quietness in deed, similarity in speech and walking; and avoid impetuous haste. For then the mind will remain steadfast, and will not be confused by your haste and so become

[9] It will be noticed that Baptism and what in the fifth century came to be called Confirmation are here united. This was the habitual early practice; for the causes of the division see J. G. Davies, "The Disintegration of the Christian Initiation Rite," *Theology,* November, 1947.

[10] For a description of the pre-Nicene Eucharist, see p. 81.

[11] This fragment, *Exhortation to Endurance* or *To the Newly Baptized,* was only discovered at the beginning of this century; its ascription to Clement is not beyond question.

> weak and devoid of practical wisdom and perceive obscurely; nor will it be worsted by gluttony, worsted by boiling rage, worsted by the other passions, lying a ready prey for them. For the mind, seated on high on a quiet throne, gazing intently at God, must govern the passions. By no means be subject to sudden bursts of temper in order that your quietness may be adorned with good proportions and your bearing may appear something divine and sacred. Be on your guard also against signs of arrogance, a haughty bearing, a high head, a dainty and lofty footstep.
>
> Let your speech be gentle to those you encounter, and your greetings kind; be modest towards women and let your gaze be diverted to the ground. Be circumspect in all your talk, and return a serviceable answer, suiting your words to your hearers' need, loud enough to be heard clearly, neither escaping the hearing of those present by being too slight nor going to excess with too great a noise.

Clement's own delivery is a practical demonstration of this precept.

> Take care never to speak what you have not previously weighed and deliberated; nor interject offhand your own words in the midst of another's; for you must listen and talk in turn, with set times for speech and for silence. Learn gladly and teach ungrudgingly; never hinder wisdom from others because of jealousy, nor stand aloof from instruction through false modesty.

There is complete quiet in the room, apart from the

humming of some flies in the heat outside, as Clement continues his address.

Do all things unto the Lord, both deeds and words, and offer up to Christ all that is yours; and turn your soul frequently to God; and learn your thought on the might of Christ as if in some harbor by the divine light of the Savior if were resting from all talk and traffic. And often by day impart your thoughts to men, but especially to God by night as well as by day: for let not much sleep prevail to hinder your prayers and hymns to God, for deep sleep is a rival of death.

Relax not the tension of your soul with feasting and license in drink, but hold that to be sufficient which is needful for the body. And do not hasten early to meals before the time for dinner has arrived, but let your dinner be a loaf, and let all the fruits of the ground and of the trees be set before you, and go to your meal with equanimity, showing no sign of ravening gluttony. Be neither a flesh eater nor a lover of wine, when no ailment leads you to it as a remedy. But instead of delights that are in these things, choose the joys that are in divine words and hymns, joys with which you are abundantly furnished by the wisdom from God; and let heavenly meditation ever conduct you upwards to heaven.

And neglect the many anxious thoughts about the body by being confident in the hopes towards God, because He will provide all necessary things for you in sufficiency: food to sustain life, covering for the body and protection against winter cold. For the whole earth and whatever it brings forth belongs to your

> King; and God tends diligently, as His own members, the bodies of those who serve Him, like His own shrines and temples.
>
> Knowing this, equip your soul to be strong even in the face of diseases; be of good courage as a man in the arena, bravest to withstand his conflicts with strength unmoved.

A stir in the attentive audience intimates to Clement the aptness of his comparison, for all of them, though they avoid the shows in the circus, are well aware that they themselves might be presented at any time as a spectacle for others.

> Be not altogether crushed in soul by grief, whether oppressive disease torments you, or any other hardship befalls, but nobly withstand the conflicts with your understanding, even in the midst of your struggles rendering thanks to God. Have pity on those who are in distress, and ask for men the succor that comes from God; for He will grant grace to His friend when he asks, and will give aid for those in distress, wishing to make His power known to men, in the hope that, when they have come to full knowledge, they may return to God and enjoy eternal blessedness when the Son of God shall come and restore good things to His own.

After the address, Clement talks with a little group of his pupils for a few minutes and then, as the last one takes his leave, he himself prepares to go out, collecting another notebook from his study and telling his wife not to expect him back until late afternoon. A few steps brings him into the Street of the Soma, named after the imposing tomb where the body of Alexander the Great, the founder of the city, is laid to rest. Clement walks beneath one of the colonnades which run the length of the street on either side and passes the mausoleum on his right. Opposite to it, standing back in its own enclosure planted with trees, is the famous museum, founded nearly five hundred years ago by Ptolemy Soter as a center for scientific research. No effort had originally been spared in its construction, and with its communal dining room, its spacious lecture halls and its broad colonnades it is well fitted to be a temple of learning. Nor is its fame without foundation and its presidency, to which the emperor himself nominates, is regarded as a key position often leading to the highest promotion.[12] It is a matter for regret to Clement, however, that its great library, which once contained over half a million volumes, was burned in Caesar's siege of the city.

Canopic Street, stretching from the Gate of the Moon on the west to the Gate of the Sun on the east, cuts across the Street of the Soma just beyond this point and Clement, as he is about to cross, has to wait a moment as slaves shouting, "Make way!" and sweating beneath their burden go past bearing a litter; its

[12] L. Julius Vestinus was first president of the museum under Hadrian and was later transferred to Rome, where he was both librarian and imperial cabinet secretary. (T. Mommsen, *The Provinces of the Roman Empire*, 1886, II, p. 273.)

curtains are drawn aside and the lady within leans forward ogling a tall young man on the pavement and scratching her head nonchalantly with a tortoiseshell pin. Clement's disgust at this blatant self-advertisement — his own wife always wears a veil when in the streets — is not dispelled by the scene which next catches his eye, for the barber's shop which faces him is crowded with fops; one is chewing mastic, another is combing his long feminine hair; a third is fondling the ornaments which, dangling from his neck, match those attached to his ankles, while a fourth is binding his locks with a fillet. They are giggling and whispering together, their shrill tones occasionally topping the noise of the traffic as they gossip with two others receiving the barbers' attention; one of them is having his surplus hair removed by pitch and the other is having his head dyed to obscure the traces of premature old age.

Clement, his ears offended by their enervated voices, his eyes by their gaudy long silk robes and his nostrils by their perfumes which emanate from every part of their persons, mutters under his beard:

"Unless you saw them naked you would suppose them to be women!"

With some relief he turns his gaze to the clean-cut soaring walls of the Caesareum, begun by Cleopatra in honor of her lover Anthony and completed by Augustus, to whom it was finally dedicated. Between the two great obelisks[13] which had been brought from Heliopolis some thirteen years before the birth of Christ, sailors are entering the open doorway, some to thank the gods for a safe return from the sea, others to seek their protection as they prepare for another voyage. But these immoral deities cannot protect them from the courtesans who loiter round the gates, their yellow hair proclaiming their profession. Their faces are masks of paint: they have massaged them with crocodile excrement, they have rubbed white lead into the cheeks, they have stained their plucked eyebrows with soot, so that to Clement's mind these "Helens," as he calls them, are little better than apes smeared with white paint.

Clement's sardonic reflection comes to an abrupt end as he finds himself walking into the midst of a group of drunkards, staggering with crowns round their necks like wine jars, and vomiting drink on one another in the name of good fellowship. His usual measured step quickens and turning rapidly to avoid them he is jostled by some others, full of their debauch, dirty, pale in the face and livid.

"It is better to make acquaintance with this sort of thing at the greatest possible distance," he thinks to himself; "at least it is an object lesson; it reminds me of the Spartans who made their slaves drunk to cure

[13] One of these "Cleopatra's Needles" now stands on the Thames Embankment, the other in Central Park.

themselves of the desire by looking at such a disgusting sight."

He makes his escape in the direction of the corn exchange, the Emporium, and in a few minutes he is walking past the impressive façade with its tall porphyry columns. Here the businessmen of Alexandria, the wealthy merchants, haggle over the price of grain, and, if their bargaining be successful, proclaim their generosity by having lascivious pictures hung in the public squares, and by inviting their hangers-on to one of their luxurious dinner parties. In the old days, before his conversion, Clement himself had been a guest at some of these banquets, though now he usually avoids them, and he recalls with some amusement one host of whom his own private opinion was that his horse, or land, or servant, or gold, was worth fifteen talents, while the man himself was dear at three coppers. He was the person who had over his door the inscription:

HERCULES, FOR VICTORY FAMED, DWELLS HERE:
LET NOTHING BAD ENTER IN

"In that case," Clement can remember his remark at the time, "how shall the master of the house go in?"

Still, what a dinner that had been! And what a menu! The old glutton seemed to have swept the world with a dragnet to gratify his jaded palate. Served on silver and gold plate, carved with knives having forged Indian steel blades and ivory handles, were lampreys from the Straits of Sicily, oysters from Abydos, sprats from Lipara, turnips from Mantinea, cockles of Methymna, turbots of Attica, peafowl of Media. As for wines, they hailed from Lesbos, Crete, Syracuse and Italy. To follow there were sweetmeats, honey cakes, sugar plums — in fine, a multitude of desserts. Oh, yes, they were completely under the dominion of the Belly-Demon and Dion Chrysostom was right in saying that Alexandrian manners were worse even than those of the Rhodians. Raising themselves on the couches, all but pitching their faces into the dishes, they besmeared their hands with the condiments and were forever reaching for the sauces. As each dish was served, they followed it round the table with greedy eyes, waiting for the moment when they could stuff both jaws at once with it, talking all the time in indistinct mouthings punctuated with foul eructations, quaffing glass after glass of wine until wracked by hiccups. The outcome of such conduct is there for everyone to see, in the feebleness of that obese old man in front of the Emporium, who is so debilitated by his excesses that he needs a whole army of slaves to push him up the steps into the building.

Clement walks along the dockside, past the grain wharves and the warehouses until he reaches the end of the Heptastadion, the dike which connects the mainland with the island of Pharos. As he looks along it, with the Great Harbor on his right and the Haven of Happy Return on his left, he cannot help admiring the white outline of the lighthouse which towers up to four hundred feet. Built by Ptolemy Philadelphus, it was dedicated in the year 279 B.C. The architect, Sostratus, an Asiatic Greek, provided it with a colonnaded court and pierced the square bottom story, where the mechanics and attendants have their quarters, with two hundred windows. On top of this is a square platform with Tritons, mermaidlike figures, at each corner. The second story is octagonal and contains a double spiral staircase; above this the circular third story terminates in the great lantern. Clement shades his eyes from the brilliant glare of the sun, reflected by the sapphire-blue sea, and looks up at the summit, where a gigantic statue of Poseidon, the god of the sea, dominates the whole building.

"A pity," he thinks, "that that lecherous old man should be commemorated in such a magnificent fashion."

The Egyptian quarter, Rhacotis, which Clement now enters, is not so crowded as the Brucheion where he himself lives; most of the people have gone to watch the races, but some shops are still open and Clement makes his way to a little bookseller's to which he pays frequent visits. Pausing on the threshold, he glances at the advertisements which are fastened to the doorposts, and notes with interest that a new edition of Plato's *Republic* is available. Around the tables a number of customers are reading passages from the books, while in one corner two men are engaged in an animated literary discussion. Clement, who has decided that he has reached an age when he must commit his teaching to writing as a remedy against forgetfulness, wants a plain papyrus roll [14] and an assistant produces several specimens for him to examine, apologizing for the meager selection as the government department in charge of the monopoly is behindhand in allotting supplies. Clement scrutinizes the samples with care; he has often seen the plant growing in the marshes near Alexandria, its stem as thick as a man's wrist and some of its shoots reaching fifteen feet in height, and he is familiar with the process whereby the pith is extracted and strips of it are fastened on top of each other with their fibers at right angles. He has therefore no difficulty in telling which are the best quality, namely, those in which the horizontal strips are the longest. He runs his finger over the surface to see if it has been well smoothed with pumice stone, and asks for two twenty-foot rolls, made up of separate sheets thirteen inches long and nine inches wide.

While the assistant goes to the back of the shop to bring them from the store, Clement picks up a copy of

[14] Codices were also in use at this period. (C. H. Roberts, "The Christian Book and the Greek Papyri," *J.T.S.*, L, July–October, 1949, pp. 155–168.)

Plato's *Republic*; it is a handsome edition, complete in purple parchment wrapper, and, although more expensive [15] than the usual run of copies Clement feels it is worth it; after handing over the money for his purchases, he places them in the fold of his toga which serves as a pocket and bids the bookseller good day.

The other customers crowd to the doorway as he goes out, for a procession is filing past on its way to the Serapeum, the temple of Serapis, god of healing. At the head is the Singer, bearing a lyre to indicate his office; behind him walks the Astrologer with a horologe and a palm in his hand. Next comes the sacred Scribe, with wings on his head, holding a book and a rule; he is followed by the Stole-keeper with the cubit of justice and the cup for libations. Behind them all comes the Prophet, with the water vase in his arms, his hair matted, his clothes squalid and tattered, and his nails like talons. Bringing up the rear is a whole collection of slaves and attendants bearing loaves of bread.

Since the Serapeum is Clement's destination also, he follows the procession down the street until they reach the temple with its porticoes and vestibules, its field and sacred grove, and its halls surrounded with pillars. The devotees of the god disappear through the doors to take up their position before the gold-embroidered veil behind which the statue of Serapis is kept amidst in-

[15] In Rome one paid six to ten sesterces for a cheap book, five denarii for a more expensive one. (Martial, I, 117, 17.)

numerable votive offerings, such as golden ears and eyes.[16] To Clement's mind the smoke-blackened image is typical of all that is worst in pagan religion, its head crowned with a *modius,* an emblem of fertility, only serving to emphasize its lewdness; and the three-headed dog, Cerberus, which stands by its right knee, calls attention to the superstitious nonsense which clouds the hope of the future. But Clement does not enter the sacred enclosure — it is the library he has come to visit and within a few minutes he is in the vestibule consulting the classified catalogues to find Apion Pleistonices, an anti-Semite,[17] but the author of a useful work entitled *The Egyptian Histories.* Noting that it is in the sixth bookcase, Clement enters the main hall where the shelves, divided into pigeonholes of various sizes according to the number of rolls in a single work, are arranged around the walls. Looking down on him from the top of the cases are portrait busts of the many celebrated authors and philosophers, copies of whose works are to be found in the library. Clement locates the sixth bookcase and, quickly running his eye along the title labels which hang down from each roll, he extracts the volume he wants and takes it to a table in the center of the room. Unfastening the bright-colored string that encircles it, he unfolds it with his right hand and places it on the reading stand which is clamped to

[16] These were the parts of the body healed by the god.

[17] He wrote a spiteful work against the Jews to which Josephus replied in his *Contra Apionem.*

the table.[18] There is no index, no punctuation, no division between the words, so that it takes Clement some time to find the passage for which he is looking; at last he is satisfied and, having made the necessary notes on his tablets, he ties up the roll and returns it to its place.

Since one of the objects of his outing has been to provide himself with exercise, Clement has taken a rather roundabout route to reach the library of the Serapeum, but now he follows a more direct way home and soon arrives back at his house. Neither of his two slaves being at hand,[19] and considering it ill-mannered to summon them by whistling, Clement goes into the kitchen to attend to his own wants and pours out for himself a cup of fresh water,[20] which is brought by channels

18 This consisted of a vertical support on top of which was a sheet of wood with a rim along the bottom and the left side; an example is figured in a bas-relief in the Lateran Museum, reproduced by O. Seyffert, *A Dictionary of Classical Antiquities,* edited by H. Nettleship and J. E. Sandys, 1895, p. 649.

19 While the Church raised no objection to the institution of slavery as such, the Christian attitude to slaves differed entirely from that of the pagan. "Implements," declares Varro, "are of three kinds: vocal, including slaves, semi-vocal, e.g. oxen, and dumb, for instance ploughs" (*De re rust.,* i, 17, 1). In contrast Clement could assert: "Slaves are men like ourselves," to whom the Golden Rule applies (*Paed.,* iii, 12); and Lactantius affirmed: "Slaves are not slaves to us. We deem them brothers after the spirit, in religion fellow servants" (*Instit.,* V, 16).

20 It will be noticed that this is the first refreshment that Clement has taken. The pagan practice was to have no breakfast, a light lunch and a very heavy dinner. Christians at this period seem to have had meals at similar times, since the Montanists were regarded as extreme in prolonging their fasts till nightfall, whereas the orthodox only abstained until the ninth hour (Tertullian, *De jejuin.,* x). Certain passages in Clement's writings, however, suggest that he himself was not accustomed to eat before the evening; cf. *Paed.,* ii, 1.

under the main streets to every house in Alexandria. During his absence, his wife, whom he now joins in her room on the other side of the courtyard, has spent her time spinning some wool and making clothes for their son; while Clement admires the results of her labor, she inspects his purchases and listens to his account of the things he has seen. Together with their son, they make a devoted family, seeking to live a social and holy life, which is based on conjugal union, the child rejoicing in his mother, the husband in his wife, she in them both, and all in God. To them marriage is not something to be lightly entered into without serious consideration, it is a vocation, a condition of life to which God calls you, for, as Clement is wont to remind his students:

"Everyone is not to marry, nor always; but there is a time when it is suitable, and a person for whom it is suitable, and an age up to which it is suitable."

He, for his part, never ceases to be thankful for his wife's constancy, for her patience and her sympathy and for her loving care if ever he is sick; while she divides her life between God and her husband, and indeed by devoting herself to him may be said to be serving God, her domestic duties and her duty to God being one and the same thing. They pray often together, they read the Scriptures together, they go to church together, striving to make their whole life an offering to God through Jesus Christ whom they believe to be truly present where two or three are gathered together in His Name. So they converse peacefully and quietly until Clement, remembering that he has a sermon still to finish, mounts the stairs which ascend to his study from one corner of the atrium.

Clement's library or study, call it what you will,[21] is a small square room, the walls of which are lined with bookcases. The projecting ivory knobs of the rollers, the book titles on their scarlet strings, and the occasional bright purple envelope of a particularly treasured papyrus, all combine to give the room a somewhat gay appearance. Putting the paper he has bought down on the table in the center, Clement extracts from one of the pigeonholes the bucket in which he keeps the collected works of Plato; opening the lid he places *The Republic* inside and returns the container to its shelf.

The pigeonholes are well filled,[22] for although Clement, as befits a Christian who has renounced the world at his Baptism, is a man of simple tastes, and although he is generous in almsgiving, he comes of a wealthy family and has enough and to spare to obtain those works indispensable to one of his profession. To the right of the door is the section for poetry, including

21 For a description of a study discovered at Herculaneum, see J. W. Clark, *The Care of Books,* 1901, pp. 23–25.

22 A very readable and exhaustive account of the probable contents of Clement's library is given by Tollinton, *Clement of Alexandria,* 1914, I, pp. 149–177.

the lyric poems of Pindar, for whom Clement has a special affection as one who recognized in God a Savior, and the epics of Homer, which he has read with enjoyment since his student days in Athens. Next are arranged the works of the dramatists, amongst whom Euripides the satirist and Menander the comic poet take first place. The works of Philo on an adjoining shelf are frequently unrolled, for he strove to reconcile Platonism and Judaism much as Clement himself is seeking to present the Christian faith in the Platonic idiom. A useful book of reference standing in the next pigeonhole is the encyclopedia of Favorinus, an extensive compilation which provides Clement with many an interesting fact to serve as an apt illustration. Then, of course, there are numerous Christian writings, such as the four Gospels, the letters of the Apostles and other treatises produced by succeeding generations; while in contrast with these are the publications of several Gnostic sects, heretical works which must be read in order to be refuted.

For the time being, however, the defense of orthodoxy must wait, since lying on the table half finished is a sermon which Clement intends to deliver at the Eucharist next Sunday. His text is taken from St. Mark's Gospel and is the story of the rich young man who asked what he must do to be saved and was told to sell all that he had and distribute it to the poor. In prosperous Alexandria this passage presents a difficult problem, especially for those who are well-to-do, since Jesus' saying seems to imply that there is no place in the Church for them; rightly or wrongly they do not see their way to abandoning their wealth and in that case what hope is there of entering the Kingdom of Heaven?

Clement sits down and thoughtfully sharpens his reed pen with a knife, while scanning what he has already written. Noting a mistake he takes his sponge to erase it and then decides that a correction in the margin will be neater and just as effective. The majority of his interpretation has already been worked out and he has argued, to his own satisfaction, that it was not material goods that the rich man was expected to cast off, rather the whole incident has to be understood in a spiritual sense: the wealth which must be rooted out and cast away is not money itself, but the love of money; it is not the external which impedes salvation but the internal, the possession of evil desires, of abundant and uncontrolled passions. Give up these and the rich man may retain his worldly goods, no longer allowing them to dominate his thoughts, but, accepting them as a trust and possession for his brother's sake rather than his own, he must devote them to the relief of the poor and to administering to the needs of the Church. Such conduct of course means a complete change of life and this is achieved by repentance.

So far so good. What next? It will not do to end here;

these earnest seekers after God must be given some encouragement to confirm their hope of salvation, some grounds for confidence that when they have repented the way will be open before them. There is, of course, the story told about the Apostle John. Yes, that is very suitable. Clement takes up his pen again:

> Here is a story concerning John the Apostle, that has been handed down and preserved in memory. For when, on the death of the tyrant, he removed from Patmos to Ephesus, he used to go off, when requested, to the neighboring districts of the Gentiles, to appoint bishops in some places, to organize whole churches in others, in others to set among the clergy one man indicated by the Spirit. He came, then, also to a certain city at no great distance. After he had set the brethren at rest on other matters, he finally looked at the bishop who presided, and, having noticed a strongly built youth of refined appearance and ardent temperament, he said:
>
> "This man I entrust to your care with all earnestness before the Church and Christ as witnesses."
>
> When the bishop accepted the trust and made all promises, the Apostle again addressed and adjured him in the same words.
>
> Then he went back to Ephesus, while the elder took home his youthful charge, brought him up, kept him by his side, cherished him and finally enlightened him by baptism. After that he relaxed his special care and guardianship, thinking that he had placed over him the perfect guard, the seal of the Lord. But the youth

had obtained his liberty too soon, and to his ruin fell in with certain idle and dissolute fellows of his own age, of evil habits. First they led him on by costly entertainments; then also they perhaps took him with them on their nightly expeditions for robbery; then they urged him to join them in some even greater crime. He, for his part, gradually became used to their life, and having quite given up hope of salvation in God he was no longer minded to commit some small offense; but, since he had lost his soul once and for all, determined to do a great thing and suffer a like fate with the rest. So he took these same companions and organized a robber band, of which he was an active chief, the most violent, bloody and cruel of them all.

Clement takes his knife and sharpens his pen again, testing the point with his finger before continuing:

Time passed, and some need having arisen, the Church again appeals to John, who, when he had set in order the business that brought him thither, said:

"Now, bishop, return us the deposit which Christ and I together entrusted to your care in the presence and with the witness of the Church over which you preside."

At first the bishop was amazed, thinking he was being falsely charged about money which he had not received; but when the Apostle said, "It is the youth and soul of our brother that I demand back," the old man heaved a sigh and even shed tears.

"That youth," he said, "is dead."

"How and by what kind of death?"

"He is dead to God," he replied, "for he turned out a wicked and depraved man, in short, a robber; and now he has deserted the Church and taken to the hills with a troop of men like himself."

The Apostle, rending his clothes and, with a loud groan, smiting his head, said:

"A fine guardian of our brother's soul it was that I left! But provide me with a horse at once, and let me have someone to lead the way."

Although this all took place over a hundred years ago, the details are very familiar to Clement; for the personal link with John is still preserved through Irenaeus, the Bishop of Lyons, a disciple of the martyr Polycarp, himself a companion of Papias the historian, to whom John was well known.

John rode from the church, just as he was; and when he came to the place and was captured by the robbers' sentry, he neither attempted to fly nor protested but cried aloud:

"To this end am I come; bring me to your leader."

The latter for a while awaited them, armed as he was; but when he recognized John approaching, he was filled with shame and turned to flee. Forgetful of his years, John followed after him with all his might, crying out:

"Why do you flee from me, child, from your own father, from this old and unarmed man? Have pity on me, my child, do not fear. You have still hopes of life,

I myself will give account to Christ for you. If need be I will willingly undergo your penalty of death, as the Lord did for us. I will give my own life in payment for yours. Stand; believe; Christ has sent me."

On hearing this the robber at first stood still with downcast eyes, then he threw away his arms, then trembled and wept bitterly. But when the old man drew near, he embraced him, pleading his cause as best he could with groans, being baptized a second time in his tears. But the Apostle gave his pledge and solemn assurance that he had found pardon for him from the Savior. Kneeling down and praying, he then brought him back to the Church. There he interceded for him with abundant prayers, helping his struggles by continual fasting, and soothed his mind with varied exhortations. Nor did he go away, as they say, until he had set him over the Church, thus affording a great example of sincere repentance and a notable token of regeneration, a trophy of a resurrection that all might see.

Just as Clement finishes the sentence there is a respectful knock at the door, and one of his slaves announces that a lady has called to see him. His visitor is no stranger as she is a member of the Church and it is only a few weeks since she asked him to be her spiritual director;[23] nor is she entirely unexpected for Clement has noticed with concern her absence from

[23] For Clement's insistence on the need for individual Christians to set over themselves "some man of God as a trainer or pilot," see *Quis Dives,* 41.

the Easter festivities and awaits an explanation, which is quickly forthcoming.[24] She is married to a wealthy merchant who so far as he is interested in religion at all follows the practice of his forefathers and worships the Olympic gods. He has no sympathy for Christianity and seems to go out of his way to hinder her religious observances; thus if it is a station day [25] he insists on having a dinner party, if it is a feast day he makes an appointment to meet her at the public baths; when she wants to visit the poor or the sick, he finds some urgent family business to occupy her; when a pilgrim calls for refreshment he is either driven away or subjected to constant abuse; if she makes the sign of the cross before going to bed, if she tries to pray, if she wants a few moments to read the Scriptures, obstacle after obstacle is placed in her path; and now to crown it all he has deliberately prevented her from coming to the service on Easter Day. Clement listens sympathetically; it is a problem, like that of the rich Christian in his sermon, with which he is only too familiar, and his advice long meditated, is expressed with little hesitation. He says:

[24] Tertullian provides a full statement of the difficulties experienced by a believer married to a pagan, and among them is the refusal of the latter to endure his wife's absence "all the night long at the paschal solemnities" (*Ad uxor.*, II, iv).

[25] From an early date the Church recognized two fast days, Wednesday and Friday, because on these days the betrayal was planned and the Crucifixion took place. Fasting was a spiritual exercise whereby Christians stood on "watch" for their Lord; hence the military word *statio* was applied to it (Tertullian, *De cor. milit.*, xi).

"The wise woman will first choose to persuade her husband to be her associate in what is conducive to happiness; that is to say, she will seek to convert him to the Way, to sanctify him, as the Apostle Paul says. To this end, it is permissible to relax some of that strictness in dress and behavior which should normally characterize the Christian woman; for example, you may adorn yourself in order to please your husband, as long as your intention is to secure his admiration and not devote yourself to mere personal display. You may also, for the same purpose, employ a few perfumes, though not too many nor those that are overpowering; again, you may wear a little jewelry, such as a signet ring, which after all is useful for sealing things which are worth keeping safe in the home. If, however, this course of action is unsuccessful, then you must try to obey your husband in everything, being especially careful to avoid anything in your domestic economy that might annoy him, never doing anything against his will except where honor and religion are involved. If matters still go from bad to worse, then there can be no question where your allegiance must finally lie: it is to God. As therefore we were first loved by Him, and took our beginning from Him, it is not reverent to consider any other thing as more venerable or more honorable. We must stretch upwards in soul, loosed from the world and from our sins, touching the earth on tiptoe so as to appear to be in the world; we must pursue holy wisdom, although this seems folly to those whose wits are whetted for wickedness. Remember that God expects the same standards of virtue from women as from men, and as you perform your domestic duties worship God in spirit and so your management will no longer be solely occupied about the house, but also about your soul."

It is some time before Clement brings his remarks to a close and then at last he dismisses her, a little more confident, a little more hopeful, and with the assurance that he will pray for her, acting as her ambassador with God.

The sermon is still unfinished, but it will have to wait till the morrow for it is nearly suppertime and Clement, closing the front door after his visitor, goes into the dining room. His son hands him the Scriptural codex from which he has been learning his daily portion and Clement satisfies himself of his proficiency. Then, after a brief prayer,[26] he reads a further passage, his wife and his two slaves, whom he treats like himself, completing the audience. Grace follows, a simple blessing of the Creator for all the fruits of the earth they are about to enjoy. Since the Christian does not live to eat but eats to live and preserve his health and strength, the meal, in contrast to the lavish banquets of the pagans, is plain and frugal. There are olives, some

[26] Origen (*De orat.*, 31) informs us that Scripture, which is to be read daily, can only be understood when preceded by prayer.

green vegetables, cheese and brown bread, the last being baked at home from flour which has not been so highly purified that it has lost all its goodness. The diet is indeed light and digestible, not the kind to make one heavy with sleep nor to induce sensual dreams in bed. The modest earthenware vessels, the plain-handled knives, the good manners so that no one speaks with his mouth full or pagan-fashion dribbles down his chin, all emphasize the restraint and simplicity which should characterize every Christian household. Clement disdains pastry, which he regards as a useless product, but partakes of some fruit and drinks a cup of water; not that he objects to wine — he is indeed an advocate of having a little with water in the evening when it is cold — but he forbids it for children and looks on water as the more natural drink.

After giving thanks to God, the family joins in a hymn, which is Clement's own composition:

Bridle of colts untamed,
  Over our wills presiding;
Wing of unwandering birds,
  Our flight securely guiding.
Rudder of youth unbending,
  Firm against adverse shock;
Shepherd with wisdom tending
  Lambs of the royal flock:
Thy simple children bring
In One, that they may sing
In solemn lays

Their hymns of praise
With guileless lips to Christ their King.

King of saints, almighty Word
Of the Father highest Lord;
Wisdom's head and chief;
Assuagement of all grief;
Lord of all time and space,
Jesus, Savior of our race;
Shepherd, who dost us keep;
  Husbandman who tillest.
Bit to restrain us, Rudder
  To guide us as Thou willest;
Of the all-holy flock celestial wing;
Fisher of men, whom Thou to life dost bring;
From evil sea of sin,
  And from the billowy strife,
Gathering pure fishes in,
  Caught with sweet bait of life:
Lead us, Shepherd of the sheep,
  Reason-gifted, holy One;
King of youths, whom Thou dost keep,
  So that they pollution shun:
Steps of Christ, celestial Way;
Word eternal, Age unending;
Life that never can decay;
  Fount of mercy, virtue-sending;
Life august of those who raise
Unto God their hymn of praise,
                    Jesus Christ.

Nourished by the milk of heaven
To our tender palates given;

Milk of wisdom from the breast
Of that bride of grace expressed;
By a dewy spirit filled
From fair Reason's breast distilled;
Let us sucklings join to raise
With pure lip our hymns of praise
As our grateful offering,
Clean and pure, to Christ our King.
Let us, with hearts undefiled,
Celebrate the mighty Child.
We, Christ-born, the choir of peace;
  We, the people of His love,
Let us sing nor ever cease,
  To the God of peace above.

The day is coming to a close and the family retire to their bedrooms to prepare for the night. Standing with his arms outstretched, Clement thanks God for his enjoyment of His grace and love, and lying down on his truckle bed, with his goat skin rug pulled up over him, he spends the few minutes before he drops off to sleep in meditation, turning in on himself, since to know oneself is to know God, illumining the eyes of the hidden man and gazing on the Truth itself. It would be a mistake, however, to think that Clement will lie here undisturbed until another day breaks. He sleeps lightly and often rises throughout the hours of darkness to bless God, sometimes taking a book from the case let into the wall and reading a few columns before returning to his couch.

As there is one mode of training for philosophers, another for orators, and another for athletes, so there is a generous disposition, suitable to the choice that is set on moral loveliness, resulting from the training of Christ. And in the case of those who have been trained according to His influence, their gait in walking, their sitting at table, their food, their sleep, their going to bed, their regimen, and the rest of their mode of life, acquires a superior dignity. We must confess, therefore, the deepest obligation to Him. For what else do we say is incumbent on the rational creature — I mean man — than the contemplation of the Divine, conforming ourselves to the Teacher, and making the word and our deeds agree, to live a real life? [27]

[27] *Paed.*, i, 12.

2

Paul, A Heretic of Antioch

A.D. 268

PAUL came into sudden prominence in the year A.D. 260 when he was consecrated Bishop of Antioch. Of his life before this date little is known, except that he was born of poor parents, that Samosata was his native city and that he himself had no trade or occupation prior to his elevation. Enjoying the patronage of Zenobia, Queen of Palmyra, he combined his episcopal office with the civil one of Procurator Ducenarius, *and the authority he thus wielded helped to protect him against the charges of heresy which were soon leveled at him. His teaching seems to have been a variety of adoptionism — the belief that Jesus was not perfect God and perfect man, but a mere man who received divine honors after his death. Two synods, presided over by Firmilian, Bishop of Caesarea in Cappadocia, held at Antioch between 264–268, achieved no result as Paul succeeded in dissembling his real beliefs. In 269, under the presidency of Helenus, Bishop of Tarsus, a third synod was held, and, due to the efforts of the presbyter Malchion, Paul was declared deposed. Protected by Zenobia, however, he remained in occupation of the episcopal residence until the defeat and capture of the queen by Aurelian in 272; this brought the meteoric career of this secular cleric, the forerunner of such men as Eusebius of Nicomedia and Theophilus of Alexandria, to an abrupt end, and he passes once more into the same obscurity which shrouds his early years — not even the date of his death is known.*

The visitor to Antioch would find it difficult to decide which is its most attractive feature — there is the broad sweep of the River Orontes, a hundred and twenty-five feet wide, skirting the northern edge of the city; there is the great main street, four and a half miles long, with handsomely adorned colonnades on either side; there are the theaters, circuses and temples, and there is the famous and lovely suburb of Daphne with its laurel groves and gushing streams. But whatever perplexity the traveler might feel in attempting to choose between these many and varied beauties, of nature and of art, he would not hesitate for a moment in declaring who is the most notable citizen, who of the half a million inhabitants is most prominent in the public eye. That person, beyond a doubt, is Paul, Paul of Samosata, the Christian bishop, and, perhaps even more important, the Procurator

Ducenarius, wielding a power in matters financial subordinate only to the will of the Queen Zenobia.

Not that one would find Paul so splendid and imposing first thing in the morning; but then, as has been said, no man is a hero to his valet, and Paul, as he rises from his feather bed, his eyes bleary with the wine of the night before, his face stretched in a gigantic yawn, is anything but the angel from heaven that his partisans are wont to declare.

Paul picks up an ivory comb and, running it through his long hair, contemplates moodily the figure of the young woman who has been sharing his couch. A dry smile crinkles his cheeks; how the moralists detest his having two such companions in the house [1] — he had a third, but grew tired of her — but then, since he permits his clergy to do the same, there are few in his diocese who dare raise a voice against him. Besides, the young need a protector, and if moral lapses occasionally occur one must not expect too much from human nature.

In response to his loud summons, a horde of slaves enters the room. One has a razor and scissors to trim his beard, another rose water to rinse his hands, a third pigment to fix his hair, while others bring his silk robes and gold-plated sandals. Paul makes his toilet leisurely, his gaze dwelling now on the painted tablets hung

[1] Such women were nicknamed "subintroduced." Cyprian condemns the practice, saying that "no one very close to danger is safe for long." (*Ep.*, IV, 2.)

above his bed with a picture of Aphrodite locked in the embrace of her paramour, now on the mosaic which adorns the floor with scenes of the Judgment of Paris and a drinking bout between Dionysius and Hercules.

"Tell me," he inquires of his steward who is in attendance, "has the workman finished that mosaic in my study?"

"Yes, sir" — the slave is eager to prove his efficiency by the promptness of his reply — "the evil eye with the trident piercing it is very finely done, and the lucky hunchback is funny enough to scare away any evil with laughter." [2]

"Hm," muses the procurator, "let us hope he does so; my brother bishops have held two synods to be rid of me, I trust we shall not have a third."

Paul ascends to the flat roof, a pleasant retreat in the gentle warmth of the early morning, and there he partakes of his breakfast — a little bread dipped in wine. The great city, stirring to life and busy activity, stretches out before him; the aristocratic west end, in which he has his palace, rises to his right to Iopolis, the first of the three hills forming the southern half of Antioch. Next to Iopolis is the Silpian hill, fifteen hundred feet high, with its free air and pleasant views, and beyond that the Stauris hill, which slopes down to

[2] A very readable account of these superstitious designs, believed to avert all forms of evil and suffering, is given by Doro Levi, "The Evil Eye and the Lucky Hunchback," *Antioch-on-the-Orontes,* III, 1941, pp. 220–232.

the eastern gate and the Vicus Agrippae beyond. Turning, Paul looks to the southwest across the gardens and rose groves, the vineyards and plantations, the fountains and baths which form part of the suburb of Heraclea, to Daphne only five miles away. His thoughts go back to former days when he frequented its pleasant groves, their cypresses and laurels so thick and interlaced that they form a roof beneath which one can enjoy to the full the temperateness of the air and the breath of the friendly winds. Here, so the legend runs, Daphne, daughter of the River Ladon, was changed into a laurel tree [3] while she was fleeing from the embraces of Apollo. In honor of the god, Seleucus, the founder of the city, built a magnificent temple, and for it the Athenian sculptor Bryaxis made a great statue of Apollo, reaching almost to the roof, of vine wood overlaid with gold, the exposed parts of the body being of white marble. The god's hair is also of gold intertwined with a golden laurel wreath, his eyes two large jacinths; he wears a long tunic, holds a sacrificial bowl in one hand, and with the other touches a harp, his mouth open as if in song.[4] With such a patron it is not surprising that Daphne has become notorious for its sexual license — indeed, anyone living here without a mistress is regarded as ungracious and shunned as one to be abhorred; it is the favorite ren-

[3] Its Greek name is *daphne*.

[4] The statue was preserved until October 22, 362, when during a visit of the Emperor Julian to the city it was destroyed by fire.

dezvous of courtesans, "practiced in intercourse like the wild boar." Since his consecration, Paul has avoided visiting it, for the conduct goes a little too far; what he himself does in private is his own concern, but as a public figure he has to exercise self-restraint to preserve his dignity and not to alienate the more pious among his congregation.

The announcement by a slave that a visitor has called interrupts Paul's reflections and since, as his namesake the Apostle wrote to Timothy, a bishop must be "given to hospitality," he dispenses with his morning prayer and descends to the ground floor, where Cassius Longinus is awaiting him.[5]

"Ah!" Paul greets his friend with a smile. "Here's our living library, or should I say walking museum?"

Longinus accepts the remark with a courtly inclination of the head as a compliment to his learning.

"And how is our beautiful queen?" asks Paul. "With her pearly white teeth and her large sparkling black eyes, eh?"

"She is well," replies the philosopher. "When I left her she was mounted for the hunt, but not too occupied to bid me good-by in Latin, Greek, Syriac and Egyptian!"

The purpose of Longinus's visit is to confer with

[5] Longinus was a famous Athenian philosopher and the teacher of the Neoplatonist Porphyry. He was summoned to Palmyra by Zenobia, to whom he acted as chief adviser, paying for his counsel by his death in 272, when Aurelian overthrew the queen.

Paul about the political situation, which is not without complexity. It is a year since the Queen's husband, Odaenathus, who successfully crushed the Persian menace of King Shaphur, was assassinated. Zenobia has so far maintained his rule, preserving her independence of Rome, and making her son Wahballath titular king in Egypt. But the death of the indolent Gallienus, also by assassination, has brought to the imperial throne a soldier, Claudius, who is not likely to leave the Palmyrenes in peace. The discussion turns on the possibility of a renewed threat from Persia, on the extent to which Arabian troops can be counted upon, and on the financial arrangements necessary to meet the increased expenditure in armaments. The last point is Paul's particular concern, since as Procurator Ducenarius it is his task to supervise the raising of the poll taxes and land taxes, and the levying of customs dues.

"We shall have to increase the taxes," concludes Paul.

"That won't be accepted any too cheerfully by the people," comments Longinus.

"If I had my way," shrugs the bishop, "I would tax their air!"

Waiting at the door for him, when the conference is over, are Paul's lictors carrying their axes enclosed in bundles of rods, the symbol of authority to which his secular office entitles him. The guard of honor is one that he is pleased to have accompany him on all possible occasions, but these are not his only attendants;

as he emerges from his house and walks along beneath the projecting latticework which in the side streets shields pedestrians from the sun or rain, he immediately becomes the center of a hustling crowd of petitioners, clients and suitors of all kinds. Here is one man with a lawsuit who is anxious to be rid of those that trouble him; while he makes the necessary financial arrangement with Paul's steward, who is also accompanying him — an arrangement which the more forthright would call a bribe — the bishop dictates a letter to his secretary, so that the man's plea may receive immediate attention. There is another who has come up from one of Paul's country estates to arrange the date of the corn harvest; since the farmer's subsistence depends upon his percentage of the produce, it is obviously to his advantage to garner the crops as late as possible; Paul, on the other hand, with an eye to business, is well aware that a premature harvest, before corn becomes plentiful, will ensure a higher price. He agrees in the end, in magnanimous fashion, to postpone the date, but he insists on receiving a payment in compensation for what he is likely to lose due to the fluctuation of the market.

The lictors clear a way through the increasing traffic into the main street, where Paul, still talking, still dictating this letter and that, saunters leisurely beneath the colonnades which are adorned with statues and bronzes, some of them covered with gold leaf. Reaching the Omphalos, a great stone with a statue of Apollo seated on it which marks the junction of the two principal streets from east to west and from north to south (the latter leading directly to the round island in the Orontes), Paul and his company turn in the direction of the forum, the chief center of business and social life at this time of the morning. Here there are shops of all kinds: fish shops, with eels from the Lake of Antioch twelve miles to the northeast, and lampreys from Seleucia, the port at the mouth of the river; oil shops, with rows upon rows of jars, brimming with the native olive oil; butchers' shops, where the men are chopping the meat on round blocks raised upon tripods.

Paul sweeps on, but not so fast that he has no time to notice the striking-looking woman with flame-colored hair, dyed with saffron, nor to appraise the coiffure of another young Syrian wench, with a bun of false hair neatly molded to the nape of the neck. "Let thine eye look straight, and thine eyelids wink right," says the Book of Proverbs, and Paul, with inquisitive glance, obeys the injunction, though hardly in the sense originally intended.

Making his way to his usual corner of the forum, Paul is greeted by a further band of sycophants and more petitioners who have been awaiting his arrival.

"I hear you are running a horse in the race tomorrow, your honor and dignity," remarks one of the wealthy citizens.

"Yes, I've had him specially imported from Spain," replies Paul, "a very fine horse, and a jockey from the town that produces the best — Laodicea; he'll take some beating I can tell you."

'Maybe," nods the man. "I think mine will give him a good race."

"Well," rejoins Paul, with a smile, for the citizen is a devotee of the sun-god, "we shall see whether Christ will beat Apollo, eh?"

He turns to supervise the checking of some goods which are liable for duty, seeing that the customs label is affixed to each before passing them for sale. Then there are some bonds to attend to, and some mortgages; he gives instructions for them to be deposited at the official registry. So the morning passes, with reading and dictating more letters, attending to petitions, regulating his own commercial affairs, his cattle breeding (of which Antioch with its rich pasture lands is a center), certain Church appointments which he is pleased to make in receipt of some little consideration, and the purchase of some furs for his lady friends.

The streets are more crowded than ever by the time Paul brings his transactions to an end. A group of burly wrestlers from Ascalon and broad-shouldered boxers from Castabala pass on their way to the Plethrium, the wrestling school near the temple of Hermes; some drunken gladiators lurch out of a nearby tavern, belching oaths and boasts; women of fashion, in their bright clothes of Sardis dye, their embroidery of gold and Indian silks, are carried past in their litters to lunch.

Paul stops at a jeweler's, near the temple of Zeus Olympus, to admire the necklaces of amethyst, ceraunites, topaz and Milesian emeralds. The trouble with having women in the house is that they are always expecting some present or other; still, he has had a successful morning and an odd gold ankle fetter or a fan will not cost too much. The jeweler, who has a flair for the literary, or at least for literary allusions which recommend his treasures, quotes glibly from Aristophanes, as he displays his gewgaws.

> Snoods, fillets, natron and steel;
> Pumice stone, band, backband,
> Back veil, paint, necklaces,
> Paints for the eyes, soft garment, hair net,
> Girdle, shawl, fine purple border,
> Long robe, tunic, Barathrum, round tunic.
> Ear pendants, jewelry, earrings;
> Mallow-colored, cluster-shaped anklets;
> Buckles, clasps, necklets,
> Fetters, seals, chains, rings, powders,
> Bosses, bands, olisbi, Sardian stones,
> Fans, helicters.

Paul laughingly disclaims the means to buy such a profusion of ornaments and finally selects some eardrops of pearl, leaving it to his steward to meet the bill.

The lunch which is awaiting him when he arrives home is a simple affair, for dinner is the main meal of the day — a salad made of garlic from Baalbek, some of the famous Syrian radishes, some Rechef onions and lettuce, cress and cucumber; with this, pure white bread and a glass of Berytus wine; as dessert there are Zoar dates and the delicious pomegranates of Geba.

A little rest is now obviously called for, and Paul goes up to the roof where a couch is placed beneath an awning. The air is pleasantly warm and heavy with the mingled scent of lilies, jacinths and pinks which rises from the many gardens of Antioch. Here, for an hour or more, Paul takes his ease, dozing comfortably, fanned by a slave if the sun penetrates too fiercely. But, agreeable though the siesta is, Paul is too busy a man to remain here for the whole afternoon, and at length he descends to his study, there to prepare a sermon for a service which he has arranged to take place later in the day.[6]

It is time, he thinks, to show his hand, to declare his beliefs in no uncertain terms; his position is safeguarded by his patroness Zenobia, and to preach the unity of God is bound to appeal to her Jewish ideas.

[6] Services were usually held in the early morning or in the evening, but Paul's liturgical innovations make this hour of service not an impossible one.

It is true that there is Malchion, head of a school of rhetoric, one of the Greek educational establishments in the city, whom Paul, in a misguided excess of tolerance, has ordained presbyter: he may carp and cavil, but what matters one individual voice among the many who will applaud him? [7]

The large house [8] in which the Christians meet for worship is next door to the episcopal residence and thither Paul repairs, notes in hand, to join his presbyters and deacons. The service is a simple one but not without its novelties; there are some readings from the Scriptures, some psalms — not however addressed to Christ, a practice the bishop has stopped on the grounds that it is a modern innovation, but addressed to himself and sung by a choir of women, whom he has specially trained. During this part of the service Paul remains, with becoming modesty, in a small withdrawing room he has had built, screened off with latticework and curtains, but when the moment for the sermon arrives he issues forth to the tumultuous applause of his partisans and takes his seat on the specially constructed lofty throne on the spacious platform at one end of the room. Surveying the congregation with lofty and disdainful eyes, the bishop waits for silence and then begins:

[7] It did matter; Malchion was the one mainly responsible for the condemnation of Paul at the third synod of 269.

[8] Eusebius calls it "the house of the assembly"; Paul seems to have been responsible for extensive architectural alterations.

There have been, during the course of the past hundred or so years, many interpreters of the Word of God, now departed this life, who have erred considerably in their exposition and have unfortunately misled many people in the true understanding of God and of Jesus Christ. First then, in order to rid ourselves of these falsehoods, let us consider the noble theme of the Godhead, and next, when that has been made evident, we will turn to the doctrine of the person of Christ.

"The Lord thy God is one Lord"—that is what the Scriptures say and nothing could be more clear. I have no time for those people who divide the Godhead, multiply gods, and declare that there is more than one Person who is God.

At this, Paul becomes so excited that he smites his thigh with his hand and stamps on the tribunal with his feet.

No, there is only one God, and He is the Father of all. At the same time we must recognize that God has had from all eternity His Reason, or Word if you prefer the term, in the same manner as a man has reason in his heart, as an element of his personality. But God's Word has no independent existence, it is impersonal as is human reason or speech.

If we accept this rational and Scriptural belief that there is one God, and that in God there is but one Person, we must also affirm that Jesus Christ was a mere man, a man like one of us.

He pauses dramatically after this unorthodox assertion, bestowing a patronizing smile on those who by their demeanor intimate acceptance of his statement and an indignant frown on those who are obviously not in agreement.

A mere man, I repeat, a being from below, not one who has come down from heaven. Yet of course he is superior to other men in all respects. How does this Come about? The Word, God's Reason, after acting upon Moses and the prophets, at length came to dwell, in an exceptional degree, as a divine power in Jesus Christ. This indwelling however does not make Jesus personally God, he is not invested with divinity, nor does it give to the Word personality; the Word is a divine attribute imparted to the son of Mary as a quality. Yet thanks to this indwelling, the life of Jesus was a continuous progress towards higher things. You see how I safeguard the uniqueness of Jesus!

At this there is a burst of applause and a waving of handkerchiefs, much to Paul's gratification.

This continuous progress of the man Jesus brought him to moral perfection, for his love of God never failed and his will was one with the will of God, so he conquered sin and established virtue. As a reward he was granted the power of working miracles and for the sufferings that he endured he received the Name that is above every name, thus attaining the titles of Redeemer and Savior of the race. It is fitting therefore that he should be regarded as God, not God by nature, but he became God by virtue, by his union with God, by absolute harmony of will, and this union is eternal and will never be dissolved.

Paul, who in his agitation has leaped to his feet, sits down again on his throne as a sign that he has finished, while his followers jump up and shout, the scene reminding one more of a theater than a church. But there are those who do not share this enthusiasm and have listened with orderly reverence; before the dismissal Paul does not lose the opportunity to rebuke and insult these lukewarm supporters for their lack of appreciation. Nevertheless, the reception of his sermon by the majority has been such as to leave him in a pleased frame of mind and it is in amiable fashion that he leaves the church and summons his slaves to escort him to the baths.

Paul, as his official position warrants, enters the baths without payment, although others, children excepted, do not enjoy this privilege. Passing through the vestibule, acknowledging ingratiating obeisance from all sides, he enters the dressing room and removes his clothes, which he leaves in the care of one of his slaves, a necessary safeguard since theft is very common. Thence he proceeds to the sweating room, where he lounges in the gold-plated seat, placed there for him at his own expense. The hot air, led from the furnace by flues into the space under the floor and round the hollow walls in earthenware pipes, produces a heavy atmosphere which soon makes him perspire. Here the licentious indulgence of the eye has no impediment, for women as well as men are sweltering their naked bodies in the steady heat; indeed through the bodies themselves the wantonness of lust shines clearly, as in the case of dropsical people, the water covered by the skin. From a nearby room they can hear the sound of a ball game, as the small hard ball is struck by the hands against the corners of a triangle, but Paul is too enervated for such activity, nor has he any desire to join his fellow citizens in the gymnasium, where they are vigorously swinging the *korykos,* a leather sack filled with sand, suspended from the ceiling.

At a word from the bishop one of his attendant slaves begins to stroke him down with the strigil, a hollow, sickle-shaped instrument which removes the dirt forced out of the pores by the perspiration. Then, sufficiently laundered, as the more astringent critics of frequent bathing call it, Paul proceeds to the warm bath with its fine mosaic floor, marble facing and gold spouts from which the water is gushing. Standing up to his knees in the shallow pools, he holds an animated conversation with one of the city councilors on the subject of the tax on slaves, while one of his own directs the flow of hot water over his body. In the tepid room, to which he next passes, Paul divides his attention between the beauty of his feminine companions and the artistry of the wall decorations until he has sufficiently cooled down to take a plunge in the cold bath. This is no place for dalliance, but it would not do to omit this bath, for the flesh, like iron, being softened by the heat needs cold to temper it and give it an edge.

In the dressing room Paul stretches himself out upon a couch, luxuriating in the pleasant sensation of being massaged, as a slave rubs oil into his arms and legs. To some, Paul is aware, it seems as if modesty is washed away in the bath, but wasn't Naaman the Syrian bidden to wash and be cleansed? Wasn't the high priest under the Old Covenant ordered to bathe himself frequently? Besides, bathing is necesary for good health and, since a Christian should be sociable, it is wrong to incarcerate oneself in a private bath, away from contact with those whom one hopes to lead eventually to some knowledge of the truth.

The air of the dressing room is filled with perfumes, for the bathers are being anointed with aloes, myrrh and scented oils which lubricate the skin and relax the nerves. But the sweet odors, redolent of licentious companionship, tend to make the head heavy, and, as oxen are pulled by rings and ropes, so is the voluptuary by fumigations and unguents. Indeed the free and easy exchange of embraces would have called forth a stern condemnation from a person less tolerant than Paul.

Refreshed, his pores now protected against the cool

evening air by the soothing oil, Paul dons his clothes and takes his leave.

Outside the gathering darkness is not noticeable for the streets are brilliantly lit with lamps hanging from the colonnades and from the façades of the houses and shops.

By the time Paul reaches his house, his guests for dinner are already arriving, accompanied by their slaves who remove their masters' shoes and lace up their sandals before withdrawing to the servants' quarters. The bishop receives them in the dining room, where his butler shows them to their places on the semicircular couch. Longinus is in the place of honor at the extreme right, Paul is opposite to him on the left. Next to Paul is one of his female companions, then a wealthy merchant from Seleucia, a city councilor, a judge, the second of the "subintroduced," a bishop who is here on a visit, and one of Paul's clients. Before the meal begins the lighting and blessing of the lamp takes place, since, although certain of the guests are not Christians, Paul expects the same tolerance he shows to them and will not therefore be deterred from carrying out certain of the practices of his religion.

When the lamp is brought in the bishop says: "The Lord be with you." "And with thy spirit." "Let us give thanks unto the Lord." "It is meet and right." "Greatness and exaltation with glory are due to him. We give thanks unto Thee, O God, because Thou hast enlightened us by revealing the incorruptible light. We therefore having finished the length of a day and having come to the beginning of the night, and having been satisfied with the light of the day which Thou didst create for our satisfaction, and since we lack not now by Thy grace a light for the evening, we sanctify Thee and we glorify Thee, world without end." "Amen."

The menu for the dinner is enough to make one's mouth water — the list of delicacies seems never-ending:

Hors d'Oeuvre

Soft-boiled eggs
Lettuce
Cabbage soused in vinegar
Cucumber
Pelorus mussels

Artichokes
Oysters
Pears cooked in oil

Jerusalem mushrooms
Asparagus
Turnips pickled in salt [9]
Olives
Cockles from Methymna

First Course

Sicilian lampreys

Sprats from Lipara
Attican turbot

Mullets from Sciathus

Mixed fish from the Jordan and the Lake of Gennezareth

Main Course

Boar's head

Third Course

Egyptian snipe
Chicken from Phasis

Median peafowl
Quail

Thrushes from Daphnis
Pheasant

[9] The turnips are tinted with various colors.

Dessert

Syrian figs	Persian nuts	Pistachios
Almonds of Perekh	Honey cakes	Sugarplums

"I must congratulate you, Paul," says Longinus, who has been admiring the sumptuous furnishings of the room, the ivory-footed couch, the splendid draperies, the fine linen tablecloth, the silver sideboard and the vessels of gold encrusted with jewels, "I must congratulate you on the taste with which you have arranged this dining room. Do you know the story of a man who visited a mansion that glistened with the great beauty of the marble and the columns? Well, when he saw the floor strewn with carpets, he spat in his host's face and excused himself by saying that there was no other place that he could do it! Needless to say," he continues amidst the general laughter, "none of us would wish to do that here since you yourself are one of the principal adornments."

Paul smilingly helps himself to some wine tempered with honey and deftly extracts a mussel with the pointed handle of his spoon.

"Have you been to see the wrestling lately?" he asks the city councilor.

"I have indeed; remarkably skilled those fellows are! There's one I saw the other day, he didn't seize his opponent upright, taking an equal advantage, but let him get a hold round his middle, and even then he threw him."

The conversation becomes general as they help themselves to the various dishes, passed to them by the attendant slaves. The merchant is discussing goats, the local breed having such long udders that he has devised a special bag to protect them against the stony ground. The judge is anxious for some inside information from Paul on the subject of tomorrow's race meeting, while the visiting bishop is paying compliments to the lady on his left.

As the second course is brought in on a magnificent three-tiered tray, one and all cannot forbear stretching forward, craning their necks like young birds from a nest, to inhale the savory aroma. They partake liberally of the sauces and the herbs — Macedonian parsley, Egyptian marjoram, Thracian thyme — sprinkling salt from the large silver saltcellar and a dash of vinegar from the crystal cruet. There is applause when the boar's head is carried in and the guests watch with admiration the deftness of the professional carver who slices the meat with rapid precision.

Paul's client, next to Longinus, is not so satisfied with his portion, for he is fobbed off with the less succulent helpings.

"Do you think this is fair?" he asks Longinus in an indignant undertone.

"No!"

"Well," asks the client, "what is your practice?"

"I treat everyone alike, for I invite people to dinner, not to an insult, and when they share my table I let them share everything."

"Your freedmen as well?"

"Yes, at such times I regard them as guests, not as freedmen."

"It must cost you a great deal," declares the client.

"Not at all."

"How can that be?"

"Because it is not a case of eating the same foods as I do, but of my eating the same food as they do."

At least there can be no complaint about the service, for the slaves are most assiduous in their attention, passing the bread, the sauces, the condiments, and pouring out water for each guest to wash his or her hands in between courses.[10]

"What pleasant conversation!" declares the merchant, taking a handful of figs.

"I agree with you," says Longinus. "Unfortunately it is not true of Antioch as a whole. Apollo would do well, sir"—he addresses the judge—"to transform your fellow-citizens as your Daphne was transformed, for while the laurels know how to whisper, men do not know how to speak."

The conclusion of the meal does not mean the end of

10 Forks and knives, though employed for serving, were not used by the diners; they fed themselves with a spoon and their fingers.

the conviviality, for it is usual to follow it with a carousal. The judge, a most suitable choice, is elected umpire, and he accordingly decides the quantity of each wine to be consumed and the proportion of warm water to be mixed with it. He supervises its filtering through a funnel and then ladles it out of the large mixing bowl. The guests must empty their glasses without taking a breath or spilling a drop as they propose toasts to one another and to absent friends. The ladies are not behindhand in quaffing their share of the "Bacchic fuel," only they use not broad drinking cups but narrow-mouthed alabaster vessels. This does not make their conduct any the more seemly, since they throw back their heads and show their necks, gulping down the wine as if to make bare all they can to their companions. Their hiccups, however, are drowned by the music provided by flute players from Heliopolis and Syrian lyre players, while Caesarean dancers divert them with their graceful and sinuous movements.

The lamps are burning low by the time that Paul is eventually carried to bed by his slaves, there to sleep off the effect of his generous hospitality and refresh himself with deep sleep for another arduous day of secular living with a veneer, a very thin veneer, of Christian devotion.

In a combat of boxers and gladiators, generally speaking, it is not because a man is strong that he gains the victory, but because he who is vanquished was a man of no strength; and indeed this very conqueror, when afterwards matched against a really powerful man, actually retires crestfallen from the contest. In precisely the same way, heresies derive such strength as they have from the infirmities of individuals — having no strength whenever they encounter a really powerful faith.[11]

[11] Tertullian, *De praescript. haeret. II.*

NOTE. It will be evident that in this chapter the accusations made against Paul by his opponents (Eusebius, *H.E.*, vii.30.1–17) are taken *au pied de la lettre.* The charges formulated by enemies are often exaggerated but, while there are grounds for thinking that in Paul's case these were not unjustified, it should be remembered that we are here concerned not solely with Paul as a historical figure but with a heretical bishop with a composite character, representative of the worldly cleric who unfortunately is no stranger in the annals of the primitive Church.

3

Victoria, A Martyr of Carthage

A.D. 304

VICTORIA was born of heathen parents at Carthage in the last quarter of the third century. Upon her conversion to Christianity she became a consecrated virgin. In January 304, when the Diocletian persecution was reaching its height, Victoria went on a visit to nearby Abitina; there, while assisting at a celebration of the Eucharist in a private house, she was arrested with forty-eight other companions. The curator conducted a preliminary inquiry in the forum, where she joyfully confessed her faith and was then dispatched with the others to Carthage to the proconsul. On February 12, 304, she was brought before Anulinus, and after cross-examination under torture was condemned to death as a Christian and executed.[1]

Carthage, February 12, 304. The time is just before dawn and the great city is still and quiet, as darkness has brought an end to the uproar of the previous day.

[1] In this composite portrait the events are fitted into one day, and for this reason the arrest is represented as taking place in Carthage.

Except for a few heaps of charred furniture in the streets, there is no trace of the scenes of destruction in which Christians have been compelled to play so unwilling a part. The three persecuting edicts of the Emperor Diocletian have given the pagan mob an opportunity to indulge its hatred of the Church, and its violence, unchecked by the police, has raged furiously. One old man was seized and ordered to deny his Lord; when he refused, he was beaten with cudgels, his face and eyes were stabbed with sharp reeds and he was taken to the suburbs and stoned to death. One woman was forced to go to the temple of Aesculapius on the Byrsa, and, when she refused to worship, was dragged on her face through the streets and her life finally ended by stoning. The houses of known believers have been attacked, many of their owners being thrown from the upper stories, their valuables looted and the rest of their goods and chattels smashed with axes or burned on the pavements. Brute force has also been accompanied with ridicule, and one individual was to be seen parading the streets carrying a placard with the inscription: "The God of the Christians, born of an ass"; this was beneath a caricature of a being with ass's ears, a hoofed foot and a book of the Scriptures in one hand,[2] clad in a toga. The main attraction at the theater too, is a farce parodying Christian beliefs. To

[2] This was a common form of abuse; in the school for court pages discovered on the Palatine hill at Rome, there is a rough drawing on the wall of a man with hand lifted in adoration of a crucified

the shouts and ribald laughter of the crowd the principal actor lies on his back as if he were ill and calls loudly for baptism, complaining that he feels heavy and wants to be made light. "How is that to be done?" ask the other performers. "Do you think we are carpenters and are going to plane you down?" "Fools," cries the chief player, "I want to die a Christian." His desire is nearer fulfillment than he suspects, for no sooner have a mock priest and an exorcist entered and baptized him than soldiers appear and carry him off to the judge to answer for his new religion, and he is condemned to death.

Although some believers have already borne witness to their faith by a martyr's death and others, weak and fearful, have given way and offered incense to the emperor's image, and others again have fled for safety into the country, there are still many undiscovered, keeping to their homes, ready to die if necessary, but not giving themselves up, as that is against the teaching of the Gospel. Such a one is Victoria, who lies in her bed in her parents' house near the forum, her sleep disturbed by vivid dreams. She finds herself in a prison and, as she looks around, Cyprian, a former Bishop of Carthage, himself martyred in the Valerian persecution, comes to the door and knocks loudly. He is dressed in a white robe without a girdle, wearing shoes of an in-

figure with an ass's head; beneath are the words "Alexamenos worships his god."

tricate pattern. He says to her: "Victoria, we are waiting for you; come." Taking hold of her by the hand, he leads her through rough and broken country until at last they arrive at an amphitheater, and Cyprian leads her into the middle of the arena, saying: "Do not be afraid; I am here with you, and I suffer with you." Then he leaves her and she sees a huge crowd waiting eagerly. She knows that she is condemned to the beasts, but she cannot understand why no animals are let loose on her. An Egyptian comes out into the arena, a hideous man, accompanied by attendants, ready to fight against her. So she is stripped and changes into a man. Her supporters begin to rub her down with oil, as is the custom before a fight, and she sees the Egyptian opposite rolling in the sand. Suddenly a man comes forward, so tall that he towers above the amphitheater itself; he is dressed in a purple robe, without a girdle, with two stripes, one on either side, running down the center of the breast, and wearing shoes made of gold and silver; he is carrying a wand, like a trainer, and a green bough bearing golden apples. He calls for silence and says: "This Egyptian, if he prevail over her, shall kill her with a sword; and if she prevail over him, she shall receive this bough." He then retires. Victoria and her opponent approach one another and begin to use their fists; her adversary tries to catch her by the heels but she keeps beating his face with her feet; then, joining her hands, linking the fingers together, she catches hold of his head and he falls on his face while she treads upon his forehead. Then the people begin to shout and her supporters sing psalms. Going up to the trainer, she receives the bough, and kissing her he says: "Peace be with you, my daughter." And she begins to go in triumph to the Gate of Life. Soon she draws near to a palace whose walls are built of light and in front of the gate four angels are waiting who clothe her in white robes. As she enters she hears the sound of many voices saying without ceasing: "Holy, holy, holy." Sitting in the same place is one having the appearance of a man, with hair as white as snow and the face of a youth. On the right and on the left are four elders, and behind them many others. She stands in wonder before the throne, and the four angels lift her up so that she may kiss Him, and He strokes her face with His hand. The other elders say to her, "Let us stand," and they stand and give the Kiss of Peace. Then the leaders add, "Go and play," and Victoria cries, "Thanks be to God, that, as I was merry in the flesh, so am I still merrier here." [3]

The sound of her own voice wakes Victoria and, seeing by the light through the window that day is breaking, she rises hastily from her couch and as she dresses herself in her simple white robe and her veil she

[3] Dreams were a constant feature of martyrdoms (see *Mart. Poly.*, IV). The account in the text is from the description recorded by Perpetua, who was martyred, also at Carthage, on March 7, 203. Though she was probably a Montanist, her dream contains the same features and symbols as those of orthodox martyrs.

murmurs softly the words of the Lord's Prayer.

Outside in the street it is still quiet, but since there is now constant danger for Christians, no matter what the hour of day or night, she hurries across the forum, hugging her loaf of bread and flask of wine closely to her, into the Via Salutaris to the house of Octavius Felix. The door opens in answer to her gentle knock and, going down the passage into the open court, she makes her way to the large room in which the faithful are gathered for the Eucharist, acknowledging the greeting of the deacon who scrutinizes her carefully as she enters.

There are some fifty people in the room, including the priest Saturninus, who is sitting in a chair behind a small table, with a deacon on either side of him. Looking round, Victoria notices that all the sextons, eight of them, are present as well as the subdeacons and some close friends of hers who live on the other side of the city.

Saturninus rises and greets the Church and then the members of the congregation salute one another with the Kiss of Peace. A white cloth is spread on the table and the two deacons stand in front of it, the one holding a silver plate and the other a two-handled cup; Victoria takes her turn in placing her bread on the salver and emptying her offering of wine into the chalice. While Saturninus adds his contribution, some water is mixed with the wine and together with the bread it is set before him on the table. Stretching his hands over them, the priest chants the great eucharistic prayer which concludes with the "Amen" of the faithful. There is a pause as Saturninus breaks one of the loaves and eats a piece and takes three sips from the cup. After the deacons have communicated in like manner, he goes round to the front of the table with the salver while a deacon stands beside him with the chalice. One by one the congregation comes forward, first to Saturninus, then moving on to his assistant. When they are back in their places the priest begins to clean the vessels; the service is almost over, there is only the dismissal to follow, when suddenly there is a loud knock on the door and an excited voice calls: "The police!" There is no chance of escape, even if they wish, for the chief magistrate, Felix, accompanied by his clerks and a policeman named Ox, has already burst into the room before a movement can be made.

"Bring out the Scriptures of your law and anything else you have here, in obedience to the edict," orders the curator.

"The Scriptures are in the hands of the readers," replies Saturninus.

"Point out the readers or send for them."

"You know who they all are."

"I do not know them."

"Your staff knows them, that is Edusius and Junius, the shorthand writers."

"Very well," says Felix, "let us leave the question of

the readers since my staff can identify them; now produce what you have here on the spot."

Saturninus sits on his throne while the search is made and an inventory drawn up:

Item. 2 gold and 6 silver cups
Item. 6 silver dishes
Item. A silver bowl
Item. 7 silver lamps
Item. 2 taper stands
Item. 7 short brass candlesticks
Item. 11 brass lamp holders with their chains
Item. 82 women's tunics [4]
Item. 38 veils
Item. 16 men's tunics
Item. 13 pairs of men's slippers
Item. 47 pairs of women's slippers
Item. 18 pairs of clogs

The magistrate, not entirely satisfied with the number of articles discovered, turns to the sextons and repeats the command to produce what they have.

"We have produced everything."

"Your answer has been taken down in evidence."

The search party now goes the round of the other rooms, finding a silver casket and a silver candlestick in the library, and four casks and six great jars in the dining room. Again Felix repeats his demand:

[4] Gregory Dix (*The Shape of the Liturgy,* 1945, p. 25) says that these and the following items of clothing, confiscated at Citra, were for baptism; while no doubt this applies to the veils, the other articles may equally well have been for distribution to the poor.

"Where are the Scriptures?"

"We are subdeacons," reply those whom he has addressed. "It is not our place to keep the books."

"Where are the readers?"

"We do not know."

"If you do not know where they are, tell me their names."

"It has already been stated that your staff know the names; in any case we are not informers. Here we stand. Condemn us to be executed."

Felix, of course, has no authority to do this and so he orders them to be put under arrest and taken to the proconsul's residence, next door to the temple of Aesculapius on the Byrsa.

By the front door a large crowd has gathered, attracted by the noise and by the smoke and flames from Saturninus's chair which, at Felix's command, has been taken outside and burned. Their appetite for blood and excitement has been by no means satisfied by their excesses of yesterday, and their cruel leering faces make Victoria cling to Saturninus's arm for protection.

"Look," jeers one, "the babe is afraid she's going to be robbed of her mother's milk."

"We're fond of you, Victoria," shouts another, "you've good manners and you're a reasonable person; you oughtn't to do this. Go and sacrifice, it's good to live and see this light."

"Yes," answers Victoria bravely, "life is good, but

there is a better life. Light is good, if it be the true Light. All around us is good and fair; we do not wish for death or hate the works of God; but there is a better world in comparison with which we despise this. You are laying a trap for us."

"Now listen to me," intervenes a man, notorious for his evil living.

"No," interrupts Saturninus, "you try to listen to me. What you know I know, but I understand some things of which you know nothing."

"When you're condemned" — it is the contractor for the public games speaking — "I shall ask to have you for my son's exhibition of gladiators."

"That is not the way to frighten me," replies Saturninus calmly.

"Victoria," calls another, "although you won't sacrifice, come with us to the temple."

"It will do your idols no good for us to go there."

"Go on, we'll persuade you."

"I wish I could persuade you to become a Christian."

This remark is greeted with general laughter.

"You won't get us to be burned alive!"

"It is much worse to be burned in everlasting fire after your death."

The party continues to make its way along the Via Salutaris somewhat slowly, for the crowd grows thicker and thicker as the news spreads that an arrest has been made.

"If they won't sacrifice, punish them," shouts a short, fat man.

"To think that a woman of gentle education should come to this," laments another.

"This education you know has brought you famine and death and all kinds of trouble," retorts Victoria.[5]

"You felt the hunger like the rest of us."

"I did, but I had hope in God." At the thought of her Savior, Victoria cannot prevent a smile coming to her lips.

"Look at her laughing!"

"What are you grinning at?"

"I am a Christian; all who believe in Christ will laugh without misgiving in eternal joy."

By this time they have reached the top of the hill and are brought to a halt in front of the Sauciolum, the criminal court. Felix, a not unkindly man, takes the opportunity to try to dissuade them.

"What harm is there in saying, 'Caesar is Lord,' and offering incense and saving your life?"

At first he receives no reply, but, upon his insisting, Victoria answers: "I do not intend to follow your advice."

This is said so decisively that Felix realizes the futility of further argument and is about to enter the court, when a young man presses through the crowd.

[5] The reference is to recent famines and plague.

It is Fortunatian, Victoria's brother, who, to her distress, shares her parents' antagonism to her religion.[6]

"Have pity on yourself, Victoria," he calls, in agitation, "and on your parents."

"My Lord Jesus told us that he that loved father or mother more than Me is not worthy of Me." [7]

"Give up this silly superstition."

"Do you see that water pot or whatever it is?" asks Victoria, pointing to a large amphora outside a shop.

"I see it."

"Can it be called by any other name than what it is?"

"No."

"So also I cannot call myself anything but what I am, a Christian."

"Think of your youth," pleads Fortunation.

"Your exhortation is cruel mockery." With this cryptic reply Victoria mounts the steps and is taken with her fellow prisoners into a side chamber where they must await trial. They are summoned in turn to the courtroom, Saturninus going first, and after what seems only a short time Victoria is called for cross-examination.

The proconsul Anulinus is seated on a lofty throne at the far end of the hall; his twelve lictors are standing around him, together with his assessors, attendants,

[6] According to tradition he was later converted and died a martyr's death.

[7] Cf. Origen, *Ad mart.*, 11, "It is the love of wife and children that fills up the measure of martyrdom."

and secretaries with their wax tablets and pencils. Victoria is brought to the bar by two soldiers and stands quietly waiting while the clerk of the court reports that she is charged with having been present at a Christian assembly contrary to the imperial edict.[8]

ANULINUS. What is your name?

VICTORIA. I am a Christian.

ANULINUS. Stop that impious language and say what your name is.

VICTORIA. I am a Christian.

ANULINUS *(to the soldiers guarding her).* Hit her on the mouth and say to her, "Do not give crooked answers."

VICTORIA. My first and chosen name is a Christian, but if you ask my secular name it is Victoria.[9]

ANULINUS. What is your condition?

VICTORIA. I am a slave.

ANULINUS *(to the clerk of the court).* Is this true?

[8] The form of the cross-examination adopted here is that found in the *acta* of the martyrs, many of which were based upon the official records of the trial; thus the Christians of Cilicia paid two hundred denarii to one of the agents of the governor's court to make a transcript of the police records of Tarachus, Probus and Andronicus, martyred in 304. (Ruinart, *Acta primorum martyrum sincera,* 1713, p. 375.)

[9] The adoption by converts of a new name at Baptism does not seem to have become a common practice until after the period of persecution. The martyrologies provide evidence of many names which are entirely secular and some martyrs went to death bearing the names of the very gods to whom they refused to sacrifice. In the fourth century, however, specifically "Christian names" were advocated by many leading Churchmen.

CLERK. No, sir.

ANULINUS. Whose slave are you?

VICTORIA. I am a slave of Christ.

ANULINUS. Who are your parents?

VICTORIA. Christ is my true father and faith is my mother; my earthly parents are away from the city.

ANULINUS. To what country do you belong?

VICTORIA. I was born in Carthage.

ANULINUS. What is your profession?

VICTORIA. I am a consecrated virgin.

ANULINUS. Explain yourself.

VICTORIA. I am a Christian and have taken a vow not to marry that I may devote myself to the service of my Lord.

ANULINUS. Then you have no children.

VICTORIA. Yes, many by God's mercy.

AN ASSESSOR. That is a Christian way of speaking. She means she has children according to the faith.

ANULINUS. Why did you tell me a lie and say you had children?

VICTORIA. Do you wish me to show that I speak the truth and not a lie? I have children according to God in many parts of the city.

ANULINUS. You are speaking like a person who has lost possession of her faculties.

VICTORIA. The Lord Jesus, whom I have received into my inmost parts, has possession of me, and speaks by me.

ANULINUS. Of course you know the commands of the emperor that all must worship the gods who govern all things; so I recommend you to agree to sacrifice.

VICTORIA. I am a Christian, I worship Christ, the Son of God, who came in the latter times for our salvation, and delivered us from the deceit of the devil; but to such idols as these I do not sacrifice. Do what you please, it is impossible for me to sacrifice to false and unreal devils, for those who sacrifice to them are like them. For as the true worshipers according to the divine instruction of the Lord, those who worship God in spirit and in truth, become like to the glory of God and are with Him immortal, sharing eternal life through the Word, so those who serve these become like the devils in their unreality, and are with them destroyed in hell. For just vengeance is taken of him who deceived man, the noblest creature of God — I mean the devil, who by his wickedness stirs men up to this. So know, proconsul, that I do not sacrifice to these.

ANULINUS. Sacrifice to the gods and be a fool no longer.

VICTORIA. The gods that have not made the heavens and the earth, even they shall perish.

ANULINUS. You must sacrifice, the emperor has commanded it.

VICTORIA. The living do not sacrifice to the dead.

ANULINUS. Do you think the gods are dead?

VICTORIA. Do you wish to be told? These gods were never even live men that they should die. Do you wish to learn that this is true? Deprive them of the honor which you think to offer to them, and you will know that they are nothing. They are but earthly material, and in time they perish. Our God is above time. He made the ages. He Himself abides immortal and eternal, the same forever, without increase or decrease; but these gods are made by men, and, as I said, are destroyed by time. Do not wonder that they utter oracles and deceive, for the devil, who fell of old from his glorious estate, in his own wickedness seeks to frustrate the fatherly love of God to man, and being hard pressed by the saints, he fights against them and prepares war against them, and foretells the same to his own; and in like manner arguing from the things that happen to us day by day, being more ancient than we are in age, his experience teaches him to predict the future mischief which he means to do. For by his denial of God he has gained a knowledge of unrighteousness, and God allows him to tempt men, and to seek to draw them away from godliness. Believe me therefore, sir, that your position is a very false one.

ANULINUS. You ought to love your sovereign, seeing

that you enjoy the advantages of the Roman laws.

VICTORIA. Who is there that loves the emperor as much as Christians do? We pray for him constantly from year's end to year's end, that he may live long, may govern his subject people with justice, and may have peace throughout his reign. We pray also for the preservation of his armies, and for the good estate of the wide world.[10]

ANULINUS. I am glad that you do, but in order that the emperor may the better recognize your loyalty, join us in offering a sacrifice to him.

VICTORIA. I pray to my Lord who is great and true for the health of the emperor; but I may not sacrifice to the emperor, and he ought never to demand it. Who would think of sacrificing to a human being?

[10] The earliest example of a Christian prayer for rulers is contained in 1 Clement: "Thou, Lord and Master, hast given to our rulers and governors upon earth the power of sovereignty through Thine excellent and unspeakable might, that we knowing the glory and honor which Thou has given them may submit ourselves unto them, in nothing resisting Thy will. Grant unto them, therefore, O Lord, health, peace, concord, stability, that they may administer the government that Thou hast given them without failure. For Thou, O heavenly Master, King of the ages, givest to the sons of men glory and honor and power over all things that are upon earth. Do Thou, Lord, direct their counsel according to that which is good and pleasing in Thy sight, that, administering in peace and gentleness with godliness the power which Thou hast given them, they may obtain Thy favor. O Thou, who art alone able to do these things, and things far more exceeding good than these for us, we praise Thee through the High Priest and Guardian of our souls, Jesus Christ, through whom be the glory and the majesty unto Thee both now and for all generations and forever and ever. Amen." (Chap. lxi.)

ANULINUS. Sacrifice or die.

VICTORIA. That is what the Dalmatian highwaymen say — they give the traveler that choice — "Your money or your life." No one that they catch asks what is fair and reasonable, but only what force his captor can command. It is the same with you. You tell us that we must either do what is wrong or perish. Justice punishes crime. If I have been guilty of any such, I condemn my own self without waiting for your sentences; but if I am led to punishment for worshiping the true God, then it is not the law that condemns me, but the arbitrary will of a judge.

ANULINUS. My commission is to enforce the edict. If therefore you show contempt you must prepare for certain punishment.

VICTORIA. And I am commanded never to deny God. If you serve a frail man of flesh, who must soon depart from this world and be food for worms, how much more ought I to obey the most mighty God, whose power endureth forever? He has Himself said, "Whosoever shall deny Me before men, him will I also deny before My Father which is in heaven."

ANULINUS. There, I always wanted to know that. You have just confessed the mistake of your persuasion and of your law. God has a son, then?

VICTORIA. Yes.

ANULINUS. What is God's son?

VICTORIA. The Word of truth and grace.

ANULINUS. Is that his name?

VICTORIA. You did not ask me about His name, but about His powers.

ANULINUS. Tell me his name.

VICTORIA. He is called Jesus Christ.

ANULINUS. Who was God's wife who bore Him this son?

VICTORIA. The processes of earthly birth are far from our ideas of the Godhead.[11] Our Scriptures say, "My heart has brought forth a good Word." The Son of God, the Word of truth, was produced from the heart of God.

ANULINUS. God has a body then?

VICTORIA. He alone knows. We have no knowledge of invisible form; we can only reverence His power and might.

ANULINUS. If God has no body, he cannot have a heart There is no such thing as perception without organs.

[11] An argument from the same analogy — from human nature to the Godhead — was advanced by Arius, whose heresy brought such confusion to the Church in the fourth century. He contended that as Jesus was the Son of God He must be younger than His Father; there was then a time when He did not exist, and so He was not truly God of God. Athanasius, Arius's great opponent, pointed out that the analogy of human birth is quite inadequate; the teaching of Origen that the generation of the Son was an eternal act safeguards the truth of His divinity, since being an eternal act it is outside time and therefore there can have been no time when He did not exist. See p. 194.

VICTORIA. Wisdom is not the product of bodily organs; it is the gift of God. A body is not necessary to thought.

ANULINUS. I will listen to you no longer. Unless you are prepared to sacrifice I will send you to a brothel.

VICTORIA. I think that you must know that the Lord has regard to men's wills. God sees the chastity of the intention. If you compel me to this, it is no sin of mine, but a thing violently inflicted on me.

ANULINUS. Do not bring shame upon your family; it is a disgrace that will never be forgotten.

VICTORIA. Christ will know how to preserve His own.

ANULINUS. Slap her sharply with the palms of your hands and say, "Do not be a fool, but sacrifice to the gods."

FORTUNATIAN *(who has pressed forward to the front of the court)*. Sir, may I be permitted to speak?

ANULINUS. Who is this man?

CLERK. The barrister Fortunatian, sir; he is the brother of the accused.

ANULINUS. He is permitted to speak.

FORTUNATIAN. My sister is not responsible for her actions, sir; she was persuaded to this in the absence of her parents and while I myself was engaged in study.

VICTORIA. I have not been persuaded; I can produce

witnesses to prove this. All that I have done is of my own free will and choice.

FORTUNATIAN. She has been driven out of her mind with subtle arguments.

VICTORIA. This is my mind; I have never changed it.

ANULINUS. Will you go with your brother Fortunatian?

VICTORIA. No, I am a Christian, and my brethren are those who keep the commandments of God.

ANULINUS. Think what is for your good, you see your brother wants to provide for your safety.

VICTORIA. I have told you my mind.

ANULINUS. You were present at this assembly?

VICTORIA. Yes.

ANULINUS. Why did you celebrate the Eucharist contrary to the imperial edict? [12]

VICTORIA. We cannot do without the Eucharist; it is a foolish question, as if anyone could be a Christian without the Eucharist! As there can be no Eucharist without Christians, so there can be no Christians without the Eucharist. It is the hope and salvation of Christians. I was at the service and celebrated it with the brethren, for I am a Christian.

ANULINUS. Give the names of your other associates.

VICTORIA. Their names are written in the heavenly book and in the pages of God. It is not for mortal eyes to behold what has been inscribed by the immortal and invisible power of God.

[12] The actual word used for Eucharist is *dominicum.*

ANULINUS. Who was it that put these ideas into your head?

VICTORIA. Almighty God.

ANULINUS. What people were those who prevailed on you to take up with this folly?

VICTORIA. Almighty God and His only-begotten Son, Our Lord Jesus Christ.

ANULINUS. Sacrifice.

VICTORIA. No.

ANULINUS. Would you like time to consider?

VICTORIA. In such a straightforward matter there is no need to think.

ANULINUS. Do you realize that I have power to torture you?

VICTORIA. My God is greater than you, so I am not afraid of your threats. He will enable me to endure whatever you inflict upon me.

ANULINUS. Knock her mouth with stones and say, "Cease your folly."

(Two torturers, stripped except for tunics, step forward; one seizes VICTORIA *by the hair, forcing her head back, the other breaks her teeth with a stone at the proconsul's command.)*

VICTORIA. My God, which is and endureth for ever, ordained that I should be born. He gave me salvation by the saving waters of Baptism. He is with me, to help me, and to strengthen His handmaid not to commit sacrilege.

ANULINUS. Hang her up on the rack by her thumbs and put weights on her feet.

VICTORIA. I am a Christian!

ANULINUS. Change your mind. What desperation is this?

VICTORIA. It is no desperation; it is the fear of the living God.

ANULINUS. Many others have sacrificed, and they are alive and in their right mind.

VICTORIA. I cannot sacrifice.

ANULINUS. I entreat you to consider a little with yourself and change your mind.

VICTORIA. Not I, sir.

ANULINUS. Why are you so bent on death?

VICTORIA. Not upon death but upon life.

ANULINUS. You are so bent on death that you make nothing of it. Sometimes when men are prosecuted for quite a small sum of money, they will brave death with the wild beasts. You are like those men.

VICTORIA. I enjoy life, but love of life does not make me afraid to die. There is nothing better than life — the life eternal, which gives immortality to the soul which has lived well.

ANULINUS. Sacrifice.

VICTORIA. I will not.

ANULINUS. Why not?

VICTORIA. Because the sacred and divine Scriptures say, "He that sacrificeth unto any god, save unto God only, he shall be utterly destroyed."

ANULINUS. Then sacrifice to God only.

VICTORIA. God does not desire such sacrifices. The Scriptures say, "To what purpose is the multitude of your sacrifices unto me? saith the Lord. I am full of the burnt offerings of rams, and the fat of lambs; and I delight not in the blood of he-goats. Offer me no fine flour."

AN ASSESSOR. Has fine flour anything to do with your case? Are you not pleading for your life?

ANULINUS. What sacrifices does God delight in?

VICTORIA. God delights in a clean heart, and in pure thoughts, and in the sacrifice of true speech.

ANULINUS. Did not Paul offer sacrifice?

VICTORIA. God forbid.

ANULINUS. Nor Moses?

VICTORIA. Only the Jews were commanded to sacrifice, to none but God, and only at Jerusalem. The Jews do wrong now, by celebrating their rites in other places.

ANULINUS. Heat some sharp nails and pierce her hands with them.

VICTORIA. Glory to Thee, O Lord Jesu Christ, that Thou hast vouchsafed to allow my hands to be nailed for Thy Name's sake.

ANULINUS. You are in such a hurry to die because you think you will suffer for a praiseworthy object.

VICTORIA. If I am permitted to suffer thus everlasting glory will await me.

ANULINUS. If you were suffering for your country and for the laws you would have everlasting praise.

VICTORIA. It is indeed for the laws I suffer, but for the laws of God.

ANULINUS. Laws which were bequeathed to you by a dead man who was crucified. See what a fool you are to make more of a dead man than of the live emperor.

VICTORIA. He died for our sins that He might bestow upon us eternal life; but He is God who endureth forever, and whosoever confesses Him shall have eternal life, and whosoever denies Him, everlasting punishment.

ANULINUS. I am sorry for you and advise you to sacrifice and live with us.

VICTORIA. If I live with you it is death to me; but if I die, I live.

ANULINUS. Scrape her sides.

A TORTURER *(as he takes the iron claw to rip open her breasts and sides)*. Before your body is marred, take my advice, you poor woman, spare yourself.

VICTORIA. I have within me the God whom I serve through Jesus Christ.

ANULINUS. Fool, do you not know that he whom you

are calling on was a man, who, under the authority of a governor called Pontius Pilate, was fastened to the cross for his crimes? Records of it are preserved.[13]

VICTORIA. Christ is God.

ANULINUS. What makes you think he is a god?

VICTORIA. He made the blind see; He cleansed the lepers, raised the dead, restored to speech the dumb, and healed many sicknesses. A woman with an issue of blood touched the hem of His garment and was made whole. After His own death He rose again; and He did many other signs and wonders besides.

ANULINUS. And God was crucified, was he?

VICTORIA. He was crucified for our salvation. He knew that He should be crucified and suffer shame, and freely gave Himself to endure all for us. The Holy Scriptures had foretold these things concerning Him — the Scriptures which the Jews think they hold, but do not.

ANULINUS. Scrape.

VICTORIA. Lord, they are writing that Thou art mine.

ANULINUS. This is only the beginning, sacrifice and spare yourself.

VICTORIA. Don't think to terrify me with words. I am

[13] The primary reference is to the forged Acts of Pilate which were issued in an attempt to discredit the historical foundation of the faith.

ready for you at every point. I wear the armor of God.

ANULINUS. Thrice-accursed creature, what armor do you wear? You are naked and all over wounds.

VICTORIA. You do not know these things. You cannot see my defense; you are blind.

ANULINUS. Have compassion on yourself and sacrifice to the gods.

VICTORIA. The best compassion I can show myself is to confess unwaveringly Our Lord Jesus Christ, the true judge, who shall come to try the deeds of all men.

ANULINUS. Put strong vinegar mixed with salt up her nostrils.

VICTORIA. Your vinegar is sweet and your salt has lost its saltness.

ANULINUS. Mix mustard and vinegar and pour it into her nostrils.

VICTORIA. Your officers are deceiving you; they gave me honey instead of vinegar.

ANULINUS You are proud.

VICTORIA. Pride is one thing and firmness is another. I speak firmly but not proudly.

ANULINUS. What makes you smile?

VICTORIA. I saw the glory of the Lord and was glad.

ANULINUS. Lash her with thongs.

VICTORIA. Glory be to Thee, O Lord.

ANULINUS. Turn her over and beat her on the belly.

VICTORIA. Lord, help Thy servant.

ANULINUS. As you beat her, say, "Christian woman, where is your helper?"

VICTORIA. He has helped me and helps me still.

ANULINUS. Rub her sides and breasts well with salt.

VICTORIA. You must rub in more salt than that if I am to keep.

ANULINUS. You will keep just as long as the execution and no longer.

VICTORIA. Thanks be to God, today I shall be in heaven.

(ANULINUS *writes on a tablet and hands it to the clerk of the court.)*

CLERK (*reading*). Victoria having confessed herself a Christian and having admitted attendance at an unlawful assembly, since after opportunity offered her of returning to the custom of the Romans she has obstinately persisted, my sentence is that she shall be given to the beasts.

VICTORIA. Present my thanks to the emperor, for he has made me a joint heir with Christ.

Victoria is taken down from the rack and carried to the nearby prison, where she is to await her final testing in the amphitheater.

As the jailer takes her to the inner ward she hears the sound of someone singing; the voice is soft and feeble, but Victoria recognizes that it belongs to Saturninus, who, although fearfully mangled and torn, is joyfully praising God, repeating again and again: "Glory be to Thee, O Lord."

The large public cell into which she is thrust is dark and evil-smelling; there are no windows, no means of ventilation; exhausted, Victoria sinks to the floor. She is too weak to crawl to Saturninus in the opposite corner, and he, his body nothing but one huge wound, is incapable of movement. For a time he is unaware of her presence, until at last she interrupts his chanting to make herself known.

"You have not sacrificed?"

"No."

"Praise be to the Father . . . the body does not feel when the mind is wholly devoted to God."

"No, sufferings borne for the Name are not torments, but soothing ointments."

"It will not be long now, my child; show yourself worthy of your sex and of your calling."

Saturninus gathers his strength to comfort her and, speaking in labored fashion, he begins:

"You are about to pass through a noble struggle, in which the living God acts the part of superintendent, in which the Holy Ghost is your trainer, in which the prize is an eternal crown of angelic essence, citizenship in heaven, glory everlasting. Therefore, your Master, Jesus Christ, who has anointed you with His Spirit, and led you to the arena, has seen fit, before the hour of final conflict, to take you from a condition of daily life, pleasant in itself, and to impose on you a harder treatment, that your strength might be the greater. For the athletes, too, are set apart to a more rigid discipline that they may have their physical powers built up. They are kept from luxury, from daintier meats, from more pleasant drinks; they are pressed, racked, worn out; the harder their labors in the preparatory training, the stronger the hope of victory. 'And they,' says the Apostle, 'that they may obtain a corruptible crown.' We, with the crown eternal in our eye, look upon what we have undergone already as our training, that at the goal of final judgment we may be brought forward well disciplined by many a trial, since virtue is built up by hardships."

Saturninus stops, gasping for breath, then, mouthing the words rather than forming them, he continues:

"Let your spirit set before itself salvation, no longer thinking of what you have been through, but of the conflict for which it is the preparation. The flesh, perhaps, will dread the merciless sword, and the lofty cross, and the rage of the wild beasts, and the most terrible of all, the flames. But let the spirit set clearly before itself how these things have been calmly endured by many. Let us who have received the first baptism also prepare for the second; this baptism of martyrdom is greater in grace, more lofty in power, more precious in honor — a baptism wherein angels baptize

— a baptism in which God and His Christ exult — a baptism after which no one sins any more — a baptism which completes the increase of our faith — a baptism which, as we withdraw from the world, immediately associates us with God. In the baptism of water is received the remission of sins, in the baptism of blood the crown of virtues."

The presbyter's voice is growing weaker; to Victoria it sounds far away and in the dank darkness of the cell it is like the summons of an invisible messenger calling out of the distance.

"The blessed Apostle Paul says, 'The sufferings of this present time are not worthy to be compared with the coming glory which shall be revealed in us.' Should we not labor to the utmost to attain such a glory that we may become friends of God, rejoicing with Christ, that after earthly tortures and punishments we may receive divine rewards, to become coheirs of Christ, to be made equal to the angels; with the patriarchs, with the apostles, with the prophets, to rejoice in the possession of the heavenly kingdom? What persecution can conquer, what torments can overcome such thoughts as these? In persecution earth is shut up but heaven is opened; antichrist is threatening, but Christ is protecting; death is brought in but immortality follows; the world is taken away from her that is killed but paradise is set forth to her restored; the life of time is extinguished but the life of eternity is realized. What a dignity it is, and what a security, to go glad from hence, to depart gloriously in the middle of afflictions and tribulations; in a moment to close the eyes with which men and the world are looked upon, and at once to open them to look upon God and Christ! Of such a blessed departure how great is the swiftness! You shall be suddenly taken away from earth, to be placed in the heavenly kingdoms. We must embrace these things in our mind and seek our Lord's help to persevere unto the end."

At length Saturninus is too feeble to continue; the strength which he has summoned for this final affirmation of triumphant faith ebbs away and he lapses into silence. Victoria, comforted by his words, rests her head against the cold wall, her eyes closed, and in a moment she is dreaming.

She sees a vast ladder of bronze reaching up to heaven, so narrow that only one person can ascend at a time; on the sides of the ladder are fastened all kinds of iron weapons. There are swords, lances, hooks, daggers, so that if anyone goes up carelessly or without looking upwards he is mangled and his flesh caught on the weapons. Just beneath the ladder there is a huge dragon, lying in wait for those going up and seeking to frighten them from making the attempt. Saturninus goes up first, and reaching the top, he turns and calls to Victoria: "Victoria, I'm waiting for you; but see that the dragon doesn't bite you." Victoria answers: "In the name of Jesus Christ, he will not hurt me." The dragon puts out his head gently, as if afraid of her, just at the foot of the ladder, and as if she were stepping onto the first rung she treads on its head. Ascending, she sees an extensive garden and in the middle a man with white hair, in the dress of a shepherd, milking sheep; and round about are thousands dressed in white. Raising his head and looking at her, the man says: "You are welcome, my child." Then he gives her a morsel of clotted milk and she receives it in her joined hands, and eats, and all those standing round say, "Amen." At the sound of this word Victoria awakes once more, with a sweet taste in her mouth.[14]

One by one the other Christians are brought in after their cross-examination; there is Hilarian, Saturninus's youngest son; Mary, his maiden sister; and Dativus, a decurion and member of the Carthaginian senate. All have been tortured, but those have suffered the least whose turn has come towards the end, when Anulinus is exhausted with the length of time taken and by his arduous efforts to overcome their apparent stubbornness. It is these who lead the others in prayer and singing, chanting passages from the Psalms which they know by heart:

They who sow in tears, shall reap in joy.

[14] This vision was one vouchsafed to St. Perpetua; the symbolism is that of the bruising of Satan, of the Good Shepherd and of the Eucharist, the last being represented several times in the catacomb frescoes by two lambs drinking milk.

As they walked, they walked and wept, casting their seeds;
But as they come again, they shall come in exultation, bearing their sheaves.

Blessed are they that are undefiled in the way,
Who walk in the law of the Lord.
Blessed are they who search His testimonies,
And seek Him out with their whole heart.

I will not fear what man can do unto me;
The Lord is my helper.

It is difficult, even impossible, to realize that this group of people consists, in the eyes of the state, of condemned criminals who must soon pay the penalty in the amphitheater for their subversive activities; there are no groans and sighs, no words of complaint, but a radiant joyfulness, giving full meaning to Tertullian's words that the blood of martyrs is the seed of the Church.

There is a noise outside the door, and the jailer appears, accompanied by an escort of soldiers. The brethren are taken outside and the march to the amphitheater, half a mile away, begins. Their progress is slow, for not only are the prisoners weak from their ordeal, but also the streets are congested with people, eager to see the Christians and heap abuse upon them. Victoria notices a young man pushing his way to the front; she recognizes him as a believer.

"Take this," he calls, offering her a small flask, "it is drugged wine; it will help you to bear it."

"We find the fire of our tortures cold," replies Victoria.

"Take it," insists the youth.

But Victoria refuses: "The hour for breaking our fast has not yet come."

At the entrance to the amphitheater orders are given that the men should be dressed as priests of Saturn and the women as devotees of Ceres.

"We came to this issue of our own free will that our liberty might not be violated," protests Saturninus. "We pledged ourselves that we might do no such thing; this was our pact with you."

The commanding officer accepts the justice of this plea and they are taken into the underground vaults without change of clothes. Here the riffraff of the town have gained admittance.

"Let 'em run the gantlet," shouts one.

"Yes, we'll make 'em pay," cries another.

The milling, blasphemous mob divides into two lines, a narrow lane between them. They are joined by the professional beast fighters with their hunting whips of cowhide, and the prisoners are forced to run between them, to be showered with lashes, blows and kicks. But there is no opportunity for further sport of this kind; the show must run to time. Victoria is stripped, except for a narrow cincture, and, after saluting the brethren with the Kiss of Peace, she is led out into the arena,[15] preceded by a herald with a board on which is written in Latin: "This is Victoria, the Christian."

The amphitheater, which is almost as large as the Colosseum at Rome, is packed with eighty thousand people. Immediately behind the podium, the stone parapet which is separated from the wooden fence surrounding the arena by a ten-foot passageway, the well-to-do and important citizens have their reserved seats; behind them the great tiers of stone benches rise to the height of three arches; the whole, in the shape of an ellipse, is composed of fifty arcades divided by pillars. Successively embellished by leading officials, there is a lavish profusion of ornaments: carved dolphins form a frieze along the handrails of the entrances and exits between the banks of seats; sculptured figures of men, animals and boats surmount each arcade; statuettes of the gods and goddesses, of Diana and Neptune, look down upon the sandy arena, which has been devised with the greatest ingenuity so that it may even be flooded with water from nearby cisterns when aquatic scenes are presented.

Victoria, having completed the circuit, is taken to a large cross, which has already been reared in the center of the arena; attendants drive nails into it and she is

15 By Roman law women were not allowed to be executed entirely nude; in the case of Christians this was evaded by giving them a mere cincture. Theonilla of Sebastia, for example, wore a girdle of wild briars.

hoisted up and attached by ropes. Meanwhile, beneath the wooden floor strewn with sand there is great activity. The beasts, three African leopards, have been forced out of their cages by burning straw, and driven, by a movable shield which prevents their turning back, along a narrow corridor and into a large well with a base that can be raised and lowered. At a signal from the keeper, the windlasses are turned and the lift rises to the surface, and the animals appear in the brilliant afternoon sun only a few feet from where Victoria is hanging. Half starved, crazy with thirst, the beasts are terrified by the uproar of the spectators and seek a way of escape. One makes for the main exit and leaps up in an effort to scale the podium, but revolving ivory wheels beat him back. The other two try to jump the wooden fence, but the net which is strung above it foils their attempts.[16] On the other side of the barrier slaves are gathered with red-hot irons which they thrust through the narrow gap at the bottom, searing the brutes and driving them towards the center. Victoria, as she has been instructed, moves her hands to attract their attention, and one of the animals reaches the platform in a bound and gives a vicious bite at her cheek, covering her face with blood.

"Bless you, well bathed! Bless you, well bathed!" howl the crowd, but their redoubled shouting cows

[16] Since both barrier and net had to be returned back to the *podium* at the two main exits, the revolving wheels were an essential safeguard.

the frightened animals and the three huddle together trying to burrow into the sand and hide themselves. Despite more burning straw and heated irons, the leopards refuse to approach Victoria again, and the proconsul orders them to be removed. From doors in the barrier a solid line of spearmen, accompanied by slaves with seven-thonged whips loaded with hard clay balls, advances upon the beasts, driving them to a suitable exit, whence they are directed back to their cages.

For a moment there is a lull in the proceedings, while Victoria is taken down and trussed in a basket. Then a mad heifer, selected to insult her sex, is released into the arena. With head down it charges at the inert woman, and thrusting with its horns tosses her wildly into the air. Falling on her back, Victoria manages to move her hand round to rearrange her cincture, and as the bronze pin with which she fastens her hair has come loose, she clips it together again, for disheveled hair is a sign of mourning and for her this is her hour of glory.

"The frying pan! The frying pan!" [17] shrieks the crowd, but Anulinus has seen enough. He orders fagots to be brought and a fire to be built.

To the majority of the audience this is only an added item in an exciting diversion; they see only a mangled

[17] An iron chair, heated red-hot, in which the prisoner was made to sit; the martyr Blandina at Lyons in 177 was placed in this before being tossed by a bull.

girl who is deservedly suffering for her pernicious beliefs. But there are those whom duty has brought to the amphitheater, fellow Christians who wish to strengthen the martyr with their prayers, who see in Victoria the Lord Himself condemned, and who, though appalled by the cruelty, rejoice that she is receiving the purple robe of the Lamb, the royal color of the earthly emperors. There is no chance now that Victoria will be taken out of the Porta Sanavivaria, the Gate of Life whence the reprieved are led to liberty; it is through the Porta Libitinensis, the Gate of Death, that she will be carried, but to her the Porta Libitinensis is indeed the Gate of Life by which she is fully persuaded she will ascend to heaven.

With an inhuman eagerness the attendants, readily assisted by the scum of the town who have gathered in the passageways, carry wood into the arena, piling it up in a circle at a little distance from the stake, so that the fire will not come into direct contact with the body and death will be prolonged.

"Leave me as I am," says Victoria, as they are about to fasten her. "He that enables me to endure the fire will enable me to remain by the stake unflinching without any safeguard." Then, looking up to heaven, she prays:

> Lord God Almighty, Father of Thy well-beloved and blessed Son, Jesus Christ, through whom we have received the knowledge of Thee, God of Angels and

> Powers and of the whole creation and of all the race of the righteous who live before Thee, I bless Thee that Thou didst deem me worthy of this day and hour, that I should take a part among the number of the martyrs in the cup of Thy Christ to the resurrection of life eternal of soul and body in incorruption of the Holy Spirit: among whom may I be accepted before Thee today a rich and acceptable sacrifice, as Thou didst foreordain and fulfill, God faithful and true. For this above all I praise Thee, I bless Thee, I glorify Thee through the Eternal and Heavenly High Priest Jesus Christ, Thy well-beloved Son, through whom to Thee with Him and the Holy Spirit be glory now and for evermore. Amen.

As she offers up the Amen and finishes the prayer, those in charge of the fire set light to it. Through the smoke and the crackling of the flames, Victoria's voice is heard for the last time on earth:

> Blessed art Thou, Lord Jesus Christ, the Son of God, because Thou hast vouchsafed to give even to me, the sinner, this part with Thee.

In the gathering dusk of evening, when the amphitheater is deserted, a little band of devout Christians enter the arena and approach the smoldering embers. Quenching with wine, which they have brought with them, the charred remains of Victoria and her companions who have suffered a similar fate in their turn, they wrap the bones in linen cloths, handling them with loving care and reverence as more valuable than precious stones. The relics are carried to a nearby cemetery, a rectangular plot of ground in which many of the faithful have been laid to rest. There they are deposited and there they will remain, but not forgotten, for when the day of their departure, of their birthday into eternity, comes round each year, the Church will celebrate the Eucharist in memory of those who have fought the good fight.

And one of the elders answered saying unto me, What are these which are arrayed in white robes? and whence came they? And I said unto him, Sir, thou knowest. And he said unto me, These are they which came out of great tribulation, and have washed their robes, and made them white in the blood of the Lamb.[18] *O Blessed Martyrs, who were proved in the fire like precious gold, clad in the breastplate of faith and the helmet of salvation, who have been crowned with a diadem and crown that fadeth not away, because they trod underfoot the head of the devil! O Blessed Martyrs, who have earned a worthy habitation in the heavens, standing at the right hand of Christ, blessing God the Father Almighty and our Lord Jesus Christ His Son! The Lord has received His Martyrs in peace for their good confession, to whom belong honor and glory forever and ever. Amen.*[19]

18 Rev. 7: 13, 14.
19 *Acta SS. Fructuosi, etc.*, vii.

4

Diogenes, A Sexton of Rome

A.D. 350

DIOGENES lived in Rome in the first half of the fourth century and spent his adult life working in the catacomb of Domitilla, of which he appears to have been the chief fossor or sexton. This is all that is known of his individual history. He is represented in a fresco, executed c. 350, in one of the subterranean chambers of the cemetery; the painting decorated the lunette above the sarcophagus in which he was presumably laid to rest. An ill-advised attempt to remove the whole picture from its position has left it partly destroyed and as such it has been reproduced by Wilpert,[1] *but fortunately an earlier drawing by Boldetti*[2] *has preserved the original design. The inscription, flanked on either side by doves, reads:*

DIOGENES · FOSSOR · IN · PACE · DEPOSITVS
OCTABV · KALENDAS · OCTOBRIS

[1] *Die Malereien der Katakomben Roms,* 1903, *Tafel* 180.
[2] *Osservazioni sopra i cimiteri dei SS. martiri,* 1720, I. p. 60.

The sexton himself is represented holding some of his tools, with others at his feet, against an architectural background which probably commemorates some of the excavations which he had personally superintended.

It is a bright summer morning in the year A.D. 350, and Diogenes rises early in his Roman house, for a funeral has been arranged, and as the one in charge of the cemetery he has to be there to see that all is in order. He washes and dresses himself and offers up his prayer of the day:

> We praise Thee, we sing hymns to Thee, we glorify Thee, we .worship Thee by Thy great High Priest; Thee who art the true God, who art the One Unbegotten, the only inaccessible Being. For Thy great glory, O Lord and heavenly King, O God the Father Almighty, O Lord God, the Father of Christ, the immaculate Lamb, who taketh away the sin of the world, receive our prayer, Thou that sittest upon the cherubim. For Thou only art holy, Thou only art the Lord Jesus, the Christ of the God of all created nature, and our King, by whom glory and honor and worship be to Thee. Amen.

After his wife has made up a parcel of food for him he places it in a deep open-necked bag and, throwing it over his shoulder, sets off. A few steps brings him to the barber's shop, where he sits, a napkin around his shoulders, while Leopardus, a fellow Christian,[3] removes the previous day's growth from his face with a razor; for, following the fashion set by the Emperor Constantine, Diogenes is clean-shaven, and while he observes the Pauline injunction to keep his hair short he has little regard for the strictures of a Clement of Alexandria on the iniquity of dispensing with a beard.

Out in the streets once again Diogenes directs his steps along the Via Appia and, turning right into the Via Ardeatina, he begins to ascend the hill, the nails of his boots grating against the stone. His long-sleeved tunic, simply decorated with the gamma cross on the hem and the shoulders, flaps around him as he walks with slightly stooping head to avoid the direct rays of the sun, for the brilliant light of the Campagna dazzles his eyes, accustomed as they are to the darkness of the catacombs. What a difference from the days of his youth under Diocletian, when the slightest suspicion that he was a Christian would have led to his certain death! Now he wears the badge of his faith and acknowledges the greetings of his fellow believers as they pass him on the road, without fear of molestation. Opposite the cemetery of Callistus, which lies to the left, he turns into the road connecting the Via Ostensis and the Via Appia and in front of him stands the entrance

[3] The epitaph of Leopardus, bearing the signs of his trade, a mirror, scissors and two razors, is in the Lateran Museum.

to the catacomb of Domitilla, of which he is the chief sexton.

Opening the door, Diogenes steps in and looks round the atrium. On his left there are several cells ornamented with red stucco traced with designs, one of which houses the archives of the corporation of fossors; [4] next to them are a circular well, a reservoir and a fountain, and a little staircase mounts to the apartment of Theodorus, the gardener. As Diogenes closes the door, Theodorus himself appears to inform him that all is ready for the funeral and that the food — bread, chicken, hare and a *pâté* — has been delivered for the agape which is to be held in the triclinium on the right, a large room with a stone bench round the walls. As they talk, Exuperantius, Hippolytus, Quintus and other sextons emerge from the entrance to the catacomb; they are wearing the exomis, a short tunic, belted at the waist, which leaves the right arm and shoulder bare. They go to the well to wash the gray stain of the tufa off their hands, drawing the water in a bucket by means of a pulley and pouring it into some shallow earthen bowls.

Then in the distance they hear the sound of singing, punctuated from time to time with great shouts of "Alleluia!" — the funeral is approaching. The sextons open the door and go into the road; from where they

[4] An inscription on the tomb of one Vincentius declares that if anyone desires to inspect the contract they are to come to the cemetery. (O. Marruchi, *Christian Epigraphy,* 1912, n. 388, p. 327.)

are standing they can see the procession as it turns out of the Via Ardeatina. At the head, flanked by acolytes swinging thuribles smoking with incense, walks the cemetery chaplain, Marcianus, who whenever there is a break in the hymns and psalms chants, "Blessed are the dead that die in the Lord," and, "I will fear no evil, for thou art with me."

The body of the deceased is carried upon a bier, supported by white-robed friends and relations; others are waving flaming torches or palm branches. Here are no pagan funeral dirge, no hireling mourners, no mercenary bearers, but a triumphal procession, for "death is swallowed up in victory." As they reach the entrance four of the sextons step forward and shoulder the bier. The body of Gentianus lies peacefully, his arms at his sides; a faint aroma of unction and perfumes, balm and myrrh, mingles with the incense, for the soul had scarcely quitted the body and the priest concluded the noble words of the *Ordo commendationis animae* when his eyes had been closed, his body had been washed and anointed and then wrapped in white linen cloths.

Marcianus intones, "Return to thy rest, O my soul," as the cortege, guided by Diogenes, traverses the atrium and proceeds down the gentle slope which opens in the hillside down into the depths of the earth. The vaulted ceiling, lighted by the burning torches, is painted with birds and intertwining grape tendrils; on the left there is a fresco of Daniel among the lions and of two people reclining at a banquet. Now the roof flattens and on either side two marble sarcophagi lie in great recesses, relics of a former age. The passage branches into four, and Diogenes leads the procession past a great staircase which communicates with the lower levels. Close at hand in a narrow corridor, beneath a wide light shaft through which the daylight filters dimly, a grave is prepared; earlier in the day the flagstone bearing the letter L, which signifies that it is an empty tomb, has been removed. The procession comes to a halt and the bier is gently lowered to the ground.

A small portable altar is now placed against the wall beneath the open grave, and in the flickering light of the torches Marcianus begins the requiem.[5] What are these people thinking as they stand here, listening to the Epistle and Gospel, moving forward to present their offerings of bread and wine, extending their hands to receive the sacrament of the Lord's Body and Blood? The Eucharistic fellowship that they are experiencing is the deepest expression of their sense of union with the departed Gentianus; death is no barrier to this inner communion. Confident that he is at peace, that he lives in God, in the glory of God, they know

[5] Requiems took place from an early date (Tertullian, *De cor. milit.*, III; *De exhort. cast.*, II; *De monog.*, X. *Cyprian, Ep.*, LXV, 2). They were held in cemeteries (*Apostolic Constitutions*, VI, 2) and at the same time as the burial (*Eusebius, Vit. Const.*, IV, 71) before the body was laid in the tomb (Aug., *Confess.* IX, 12).

that he "is not lost, but gone before,"[6] and that this is his birthday, the day on which he is born into eternity. They moderate their natural human grief and lift up their hearts because, as Jerome expresses it, "under Jesus, that is, under the Gospel of Christ, who has unlocked for us the gate of paradise, death is accompanied not with sorrow but with joy," since "Christ has broken open the door of paradise, and quenched with blood the flaming sword and the whirling of the guardian cherubim."[7]

The Eucharist is ended and Marcianus, reverently approaching the motionless body, salutes it with the final Kiss of Peace. Then the body, enveloped in a white shroud, is gently lifted into the rectangular opening in the wall and, as the sextons cover it with a thin layer of lime, Marcianus, his arms extended, prays for the repose of the departed:

> O God, who hast authority of life and death, God of the spirits and Master of all flesh, God who killest and makest alive, who bringest down to the gates of Hades and bringest up, who createst the spirit of man within him and takest to Thyself the souls of the saints and givest rest, who alterest and changest and transformest Thy creatures, as is right and expedient, being Thyself alone incorruptible, unalterable and eternal, we beseech Thee for the repose and rest of this Thy servant: give rest to his soul, his spirit, in green places,

[6] Cyprian, *De mortalit.*, XX.
[7] Jerome, *Ep.*, XXXIX.

in chambers of rest with Abraham and Isaac and Jacob and all Thy saints: and raise up his body in the day that Thou hast ordained, according to Thy promises which cannot lie, that Thou mayest render to it also the heritage of which it is worthy in Thy holy pastures. Remember not his transgressions and sins: and cause his going forth to be peaceable and blessed. Heal the griefs of those that pertain to him with the spirit of consolation, and grant unto us all a good end through Thy only-begotten Jesus Christ, through whom to Thee is the glory and the strength in Holy Spirit to the ages of ages.

After the solemn Amen, friends and relatives step forward and strew the body with flowers, representing the joyful garden of paradise, where they are confident that the soul of Gentianus is now enjoying refreshment. Then, as the chaplain begins to read from the Scriptures, the sextons quietly and efficiently close the grave. A groove or mortise, cut in the rock, runs along the top and bottom of the cavity; into this Exuperantius and Quintus fit three tiles, bedding them in a layer of mortar. The epitaph itself is not ready, and so fragments of an ancient inscription, retrieved from a pile of debris in a distant corner of the catacomb, are inserted, deliberately arranged in their wrong order to render later identification the more easy,[8] and so there

[8] Sometimes the sextons forgot to remove this temporary covering; cf. the epitaph of Filumena (Marruchi, *Christian Epigraphy,* 1912, n. 7, p. 78).

may be no possibility of mistake, one of the relatives hands Quintus a small vase containing flowers, which he embeds in the hardening mortar, its neck inclined upwards so that the flowers and water may be renewed.

The mourners, if that be the correct word when quiet joy is the predominant note, retrace their steps towards the atrium, where they will enter the triclinium for the agape. The sextons, although invited, must continue their work, for there is much to do, and Diogenes's first task is to be present at the signing of a contract for the purchase of a tomb. Already Lucius Faustinus, the prospective buyer, is discussing it with the sexton Julius, who owns the chamber in which he desires his grave to be excavated,[9] and when Diogenes, accompanied by the chaplain Marcianus, the chief witness, joins them, they move along the corridor to the place agreed on. Faustinus wants an *arcosolium,* a recessed tomb with an arch above it, and it is to be a double tomb, for himself and his wife. The price is finally settled at one and a half solidi,[10] and Julius takes out some charcoal to mark out the semicircular open-

9 That sextons were the owners of tombs is evident from an inscription which declares that the grave has been purchased from the sexton's family. (Marruchi, *Christian Epigraphy,* 1912, n. 403, p. 335.)

10 The sextons received their stipend from the Church, and, although at first they provided tombs free of charge, later they were allowed to supplement their income by the sale of graves. Numerous inscriptions record the prices paid. Thus two solidi were paid for a *bisomus "in luminare maiore"* (near a large light shaft); the price of another was fifteen hundred folles, and the price even went as high as six solidi. The solidus was the same as the aureus and was equivalent to twenty-five denarii, which would make it worth more

ing on the wall. After writing the word *arcosolium,* followed by Faustinus's name in bold letters, he draws the base line and then begins to trace the arc. His first attempt however is not very successful and the line, the charcoal being diverted on the rough surface, bends too sharply and goes through the initial letter of *arcosolium;* [11] so Diogenes offers him his compass and Julius, opening the long arms and placing it in position, rectifies the error with a wide sweep. The site having thus been chosen and duly marked, the four men set off for the office in the vestibule.

In the cell where the archives are kept, the contract is ready for signature. It is a straightforward document, containing the names of the parties concerned: L. Faustinus and Julius; the name of the witness: the presbyter Marcianus; the price: one and a half solidi; and the exact location of the site — *undecima crypta, pila secunda, Faustini* (the tomb of Faustinus, in the eleventh gallery, on the second wall).

When the chaplain and Faustinus have gone to join in the festivities of the agape, Diogenes changes into his exomis, hurriedly eats a piece of bread, which he washes down with some water drawn from the well, and collects his tools. He takes his earthenware lamp and, solemnly making the sign of the cross, he lights

than three dollars in gold. The price of the tombs varied according to their situation and size.

[11] In the catacomb of Callistus there is an *arcosolium* unexcavated and the mistake described above has been made in the marking out.

the wick, breathing a simple prayer to His Lord who is the Light of the World, and then he descends into the catacomb once again.

His first duty as foreman is to give advice about some further excavations that are to be made on the third level of the cemetery, and going down the staircase, he threads his way through the criss-crossing corridors, so familiar with every corner that he does not even have to pause at the crossroads, until he arrives at the place where a gang of sextons is awaiting his instructions. He has conducted a preliminary survey the day before and has studied the nature of the soil, the strength of its resistance, and the relation of the proposed new gallery to the other levels.[12] He is rather doubtful whether this excavation will be a success, for they have in front of them a solid face of pozzuolana, a sandy stratum of volcanic ashes, but as they are short of space they have no alternative but to try and extend wherever there seems the slightest possibility. He tells them to drive a shaft vertically downwards for several yards, protecting the walls of it with brickwork to avoid a collapse; if the stratum seems of great depth, they are then to change their direction and excavate a horizontal passage; if they still fail to come across any granular tufa they should make a further narrow experimental cleft before finally abandoning the project.[13]

12 Spirit levels were used to ensure that the galleries were separate.

13 An experimental excavation following this exact plan is to be seen in the catacomb of Callistus.

Diogenes stands watching them for a moment as they begin their work, each one swinging his *ascia fossoria,* a long-handled pick with a curved and rounded blade, and then he turns along one of the galleries.

On either side of him the tiny flame of his lamp illuminates the neat rows of graves; suddenly he stops and looks in surprise at one of the inscriptions. He has passed here many times before, but this is the first occasion on which he has noticed anything peculiar about this slab. What is wrong? He reads it carefully, and then realizes that a word has been omitted by the engraver, so that as it stands the epitaph does not make sense. It consists of two lines of dedication, declaring that Pancratus has erected this in memory of his good wife, but the word "wife" is missing. Diogenes examines the stone, tapping it to gauge its thickness, and, concluding that it is too thin for the use of a chisel on it where it is, he takes a piece of charcoal from his pocket and prints the word in the space at the bottom.[14] As he continues his way Diogenes recalls another mistake which he noticed a few weeks ago; a slab had been cemented into place upside down, and he had scratched a dove, the symbol of peace, on it so as to partly rectify the error.

Reaching the place where he himself is engaged in excavation, he takes the spike from which his lamp is

[14] This epitaph, corrected, is still to be seen in the catacomb of Domitilla.

hanging by a chain, and drives it into the tufa wall, and then selects his tools from the bundle he has dropped on the floor. This contains several different implements whose use depends upon the nature of the soil to be removed. As the face is hard, he takes up a *dolabra fossoria,* which has a long wooden handle and a metal head, with a slightly curved point on one side and a well-tempered blade on the other. Holding it in both hands, he lifts it above his head and brings the spike down with great force into the earth, each stroke leaving a deep cut parallel with the layers of the stratum; then reversing it, so that the blade descends foremost, Diogenes hacks out the great block which his first blows have undercut, stepping smartly to one side to avoid its crushing his legs as it falls with a shower of dry particles. With a spade, he piles the debris at some distance from where he is working, resting his foot on the transverse bar which is just above the semicircular iron end. After penetrating a little way, he reaches a vein of lithoid tufa, the rock used for building purposes, and he attacks this with his *securis,* a type of pickax or mattock with a single curved blade.[15] Fortunately the vein is quite shallow and, having cleared it away, he extracts from his bundle an *ascia,* which like the *dolabra* has a long wooden handle, but its metal head consists of a hammer and a narrow

[15] This is the implement which Diogenes is depicted carrying in the fresco.

blade; with the hammer Diogenes cracks the friable tufa and uses the blade to shave off the broken-up surface. This method of working is quicker, and he soon reaches the required depth. A second *ascia* is now employed, with a short handle and a very wide blade to trim off the uneven projections, and Diogenes pauses occasionally to check with a plumb line, which is a cylindrical metal weight attached by a staple to a long piece of cord. To reach the top of the twelve-foot face, he brings a ladder, and standing on the uppermost rung he carves out the vaulting.

Glancing at his hourglass [16] he sees that it is nearly time for lunch, but he decides to mark out the first grave before leaving. With the aid of his ruler, a thin strip of wood on which the graduations are marked in red ocher, and a set square, Diogenes traces two vertical lines six feet apart, and joins them at the top and bottom, thus completing a rectangle. Then he draws ten horizontal lines at differing intervals, so that the figure is divided into six large and five smaller rectangles. The former are to be excavated as graves and the latter are the divisions between them.[17] Diogenes

[16] There is no evidence for this statement. That the sextons must have had some means of telling the time is obvious, but how they did so is not known. The Romans used the solarium, or sundial, by day, and the clepsydra by night; the latter was a glass instrument filled with water which steadily dripped away. It is not unlikely that the sextons had clepsydras, for, although no examples have been found in the catacombs, this is only to be expected in view of the fragile nature of the material.

[17] This preliminary plan, untouched, has been found in the catacomb of Cyriaca.

stands back to survey his morning's work, and feeling that he has made good progress he shoulders his tools and, taking down his lamp, he proceeds to the large unoccupied chamber nearby where he has arranged to meet some of the other sextons for their midday break.

Diogenes is the first to arrive and, while awaiting the others, he passes the time idly sketching on the wall with a piece of charcoal. His hands, which have been gripping his tools so firmly, shake a little and not even he himself would call his drawings works of art, but they amuse him and express his ideas as they pass through his mind.

Working here among the numberless bodies of those who rest in Christ,[18] the thought of the resurrection is naturally often uppermost, and so he tries his hand at the Raising of Lazarus, depicting him as a diminutive mummified figure standing before the entrance of a templelike tomb. Did not Our Lord liken His own death and resurrection to the adventures of Jonah? And so Diogenes portrays the prophet being thrown into the sea and swallowed by the monster. Pleased with the result, he roughs in the companion picture, Jonah restored and reclining under the gourd. His mind now turns to Gentianus, at whose funeral he has assisted only a few hours before; Gentianus is now in

[18] It is almost impossible to conjecture the number of Christians buried in the catacombs; the number has been put as high as a million.

the garden of paradise, and Diogenes seems to hear the deep voice of the priest murmuring:

Libera, Domine, animam ejus,
sicut liberasti Isaac de hostia, et de manu patris suae Abrahae,
sicut liberasti tres pueros de camino ignis ardentis et de manu regis iniqui . . .

And so he outlines a tiny figure to represent Isaac and a bearded armed old man as his father, and below them the Three Children in the fiery furnace. Diogenes continues to reflect upon the funeral, and he recalls how striking the procession was and how unlike those pagan burials of which he was so often a witness in his younger days. Those were days well past, days of persecution, of fear and torture, and yet the joy when the emperor had proclaimed peace was not to be forgotten. What fun it had been pulling down the statues in the forum! Diogenes grips the charcoal firmly and sketches a figure on a pedestal, holding a scepter in one hand and a patera in the other; to its right he adds a person throwing stones, and to its left a man pulling a rope which is fastened around the statue's neck. Yes, he'd seen that happening often after the Peace.[19] The sound of voices interrupts his reminiscences and he turns to greet Hilarius, Severus and Laurentius.

The four men stand in a small circle, their hands ex-

[19] These "doodles" are to be seen on the wall of a cubiculum in the cemetery of Hermes on the Via Salaria vetus.

tended, living models of the *orantes* [20] which adorn so many of the tombs around them, and then, their prayer concluded, they solemnly make the sign of the cross and squat on the floor. Diogenes takes his food from the bottom of the bag, and placing a piece of cheese on his bread he sprinkles it with salt and munches slowly. Laurentius reports that he has noticed one of the walls in the gallery near the Ampliatus vault starting to sweat; Diogenes questions him as to the extent of the moisture and directs them as their first task after lunch to see that the channels which run along each side of the gallery are cleared of any obstruction. This is a matter which requires constant attention, for, although the granular tufa is porous so that the passages and chambers are usually dry and wholesome, there is always the danger of an inundation, and a carefully planned system of slopes and gutters prevents any collection of water which may cause the walls to collapse.

Diogenes helps himself to a drink of water from the large jug which stands in one corner of the chamber, and reminds the others that the carter will be at the gate in the late afternoon to remove some of the earth which they have been excavating. For a while they sit quietly resting but, reminded by the hourglass that it is already past the seventh hour of the day, they move off to attend to their several duties.

[20] The *orans,* a figure with hands extended as if in prayer, was a popular symbol of the departed soul.

Diogenes has to inspect a chamber where the decorators are at work, and, leaving his lamp on a bracket outside, he stands in the doorway chatting with the artist, who is studying his catalogue of models. Inside the chamber the plasterers are standing on a platform supported by a scaffolding of trestles. The wall has already been prepared, having been covered with T-shaped nails; around these the workmen are heaping the plaster, which they scoop out of round buckets with their small pointed trowels. Draped from head to foot in long smocks, which protect their clothes from splashes of the liquid mixture, they are applying the first coating with great speed, for the second has to be put on before the uneven primary facing has dried. As the wall is to have paintings on it, lime and chalk worked to a smooth surface with large wooden trowels will be put on last.[21]

The artist, in answer to an inquiry from Diogenes, describes what subjects he is proposing to paint. His intention is to have on the roof a central medallion, containing the judgment by Our Lord of two of the departed, from which there are to radiate ten unequal compartments, five of them decorated with scenes and the intermediary divisions with a repeat design of a peacock and scrolls. The first scene is to be of Moses striking the rock, to remind the spectator of that Bap-

[21] This scene, exactly as described, is depicted on a Roman bas-relief.

tism by which both he and the deceased became members of the Body of Christ. Then will follow the multiplication of the loaves, typifying the Eucharist. Next, the sacrifice of Isaac; Abraham will be placed in the center with his son on his right, and to balance the kneeling figure of the child an altar with fire upon it and the divine hand reaching down from the sky. The Three Holy Children in the furnace, emphasizing the deliverance of the believer from dangers, whether in life or death, are to be drawn next with arms extended like the *orantes*. To complete the cycle, the Church and the peace which she conveys will be symbolized by Noah in the ark welcoming the return of the dove. There remain the walls and in particular two *arcosolia*, one on either side of the entrance door. The family that has purchased the first of these has already signified its wishes; they want a figure of an *orans*, representing the soul of their deceased relative, and in addition Adam and Eve, flanked by the paralytic carrying his bed. Over the left-hand tomb the artist intends to paint Daniel among the lions, and on each side of him one of the saints. Diogenes listens thoughtfully to this description and finds no fault with it; then, remembering that there is one further matter requiring his attention before he leaves, he steps out into the corridor.

The bodies that occupy this chamber have been recently carried here from provisional tombs where they have been awaiting the completion of their final resting place, and since the epitaphs are not yet ready Diogenes puts up a list of their names on the outside wall near the door. Using the blunt end of his knife, he carefully inscribes them in the plaster, which is still soft.[22]

FELICITAS	PRISCIANI
MERCURES	AGAPITI
MARCELINI	CRESCENTIONIS
IOVINI	BONOSES
CRESCENTI	PRISCILES

Diogenes now directs his steps towards the atrium, as he plans to spend the next few hours engraving some of the epitaphs for which there are a large number of orders. Blinking a little as he comes into the full light of day, he snuffs his lamp and goes to one of the little cells which is his workshop.[23]

Against the wall, slabs of marble and terra-cotta tiles are leaning. On a bench in the center of the room are Diogenes's tools — chisels, rulers, a compass, a hammer and a brush. Clearing a space, he selects a marble panel three feet long and one foot wide, and lays it down flat. After consulting his notes as to the exact

[22] This list is to be found in the catacomb of Callistus.

[23] That the sextons also included engraving among their duties may be concluded both from the implements depicted in the fresco of Diogenes and from the large number of sextons' epitaphs which, since they were not rich, they must have executed themselves; unless, as Professor Greenslade has suggested to me, these epitaphs were provided free, as a perquisite.

wording required, he takes his ruler and with the brush, which he dips in a little pot, he marks out eight horizontal lines to ensure the letters all being of uniform height. Then, putting the ruler on one side, he begins to paint in the letters, starting with the name of the deceased — GENTIANVS. Leaving a little space, he adds the word FIDELIS to indicate that Gentianus was a full member of the Church, whose prayers accompany him to where he rests IN PACE. His age follows, and Diogenes paints QVI VIX — only to decide that the general effect will be better if he puts the final syllable on the second line. He lived twenty-one years, eight months (Diogenes abbreviates MENSS), sixteen days. There remains the pious request of Gentianus's relatives that he should remember them in his prayers, because they know he lives in Christ. Diogenes fits this into two lines, representing the name of Christ by the sacred monogram. The epitaph thus sketched now reads:

GENTIANVS FIDELIS IN PACE QVI VIX
IT ANNIS XXI MENSS VIII DIES
XVI ET IN ORATIONIS TVIS
ROGES PRO NOBIS QVIA SCIMVS TE IN CHRISTVM

Diogenes considers it and, deciding that the spacing is neat and satisfactory, he takes up his hammer and chisel and with gentle taps he incises the surface, carving out shallow furrows.

It is several hours later and the sun is beginning to set across the Tiber behind the Mons Janiculus when Diogenes, still engrossed in his chiseling, is disturbed by the sound of a cart coming to a standstill outside the gate. It is the contractor arriving to take away some of the pozzuolana which has been dug out of the new gallery. He has not been able to come before as from sunrise to nearly dusk no transport is permitted in the city. While Theodorus opens the door to him, Diogenes, leaving his workshop, goes to the descent into the catacomb to summon the sextons, but he does not need to go far as they are already appearing, each one carrying on his shoulder a cane basket filled with sand and rubble.[24] Not all of the debris can be disposed of so easily; pozzuolana, which is used for cement, can be sold to the builders, but the granular tufa is not wanted by anyone, being too soft for constructional purposes, and it is often dumped in old disused galleries, especially if any of them are in danger of collapse and need strengthening.

One by one the sextons tip the contents of their baskets into the cart, stacking them up when empty in a corner of the atrium, and, as the vehicle creaks and groans on its way down the road, they stand in little groups chatting. One matter of business remains to be settled before they can go home, and at a sign

[24] This slightly conical-shaped basket is figured on the Arch of Titus.

from Diogenes they crowd into the triclinium, sitting on the stone benches round the walls and eyeing the garlands which festoon the ceiling and which have not yet been taken down after the agape.

Diogenes, standing, explains the purpose of the meeting in a short speech. One of the sextons has been guilty of conduct not becoming a member of the corporation; Diogenes has discussed the matter with the ecclesiastical authorities, in particular with Marcianus, the cemetery chaplain, and the only course open to them is to impose the severest penalty. There is some discussion; the accused makes his defense; but the general consensus of opinion is that he is guilty. After praying for the offender, Diogenes accordingly passes sentence, declaring that he is to be expelled from the corporation of sextons and that his name is to be erased from any inscriptions on which it may appear.[25]

The day's work is now over and, bidding good night to Theodorus, Diogenes sets off on his journey home, accompanied by Exuperantius. They are in a hurry, for the baths close at sunset, and having waited for the contractor they are later than usual. Entering the city by the Porta Ardeatina, they bear left until they reach the Vicus Piscinae Publicae, and passing the Circus, which surrounded with scaffolding is still in the process of restoration, they skirt the Palatine Hill and enter

25 Two inscriptions with the name of the sexton effaced are discussed in *Nuovo bullettino di arch. crist.*, 1900, pp. 127–141; cf. *Nuovo bullettino di arch. crist.*, 1888–1889, p. 140.

the forum. Pushing their way through the crowd they mount the Vicus Longus to the entrance of the baths which the Emperor Constantine himself had opened.

It does not take them long to remove their tunics in the dressing room, and within a few minutes they are sitting in one of the sweating rooms.[26] Already heated by their brisk walk, they soon begin to perspire, and they take turns in scraping one another with a strigil (for they cannot afford the luxury of an attendant, nor have they the time to laze in the hot-air chamber) and sprinkle themselves with hot water from a tub. Satisfied that most of the grime of the day's toil has been removed, Diogenes and Exuperantius with Spartanlike toughness go straight to the cold room, denying themselves the more gentle method of cooling off slowly in the tepid room, and plunge into the cold pool. After a hard rubdown with a towel they don their clothes again, and much refreshed saunter through the gathering darkness to their homes.

Diogenes's wife greets him as he enters the house, and they stand together praying, for should not Christians pray when they enter from the street, "before they sit down, and not give the frail body rest until

26 The public baths were frequently centers of immorality, but Christians were not forbidden to frequent them (Tertullian, *Apol.*, xlii; Clement, *Paed.*, III, 9; Eusebius, *Historia ecclesiastica*, V, 1; Aug., *Confess.* IX, 12) as long as they avoided mixed bathing (*lavacra mixta*) (Ambrose, *De off.*, i, 18). Chrysostom refused to use them and bathed at home, while some bishops built baths adjoining the church, as Placcus did at Gerasa, 454–455.

the soul is fed"? The evening meal is ready and Diogenes says grace:

> Thou art blessed, O Lord, who nourishest me from my youth, who givest food to all flesh. Fill our hearts with joy and gladness, that having always what is sufficient for us, we may abound to every good work, in Christ Jesus our Lord, through whom glory and honor and power be to Thee, forever. Amen.

Diogenes has a hearty appetite after his day's work and eats with gusto the plate of beans and fish which is set before him. He has no time nor money for the luxuries of the rich pagans; not for him the plump turtledoves and blackcock from Ionia, nor the mullet and scar on which they gorge themselves. He has no rich sauces and luscious wines, but bread and water, and each time he empties his glass Diogenes invokes the name of Christ instead of belching out bawdy toasts. To follow, after some cheese, they have not dried figs and pistachios, but a few sweet apples which a cousin from the Campagna has brought with him the day before.

As they eat Diogenes tells his wife how he has spent the day, describing the joy of the funeral and the peace of the requiem; then, the meal finished, he returns thanks to the Creator for the bounties they have enjoyed, and they retire to another room to await the arrival of their friends. Their pagan neighbors will be now thronging the fora and gossiping about everything under the sun, while others will be gambling, naming their stakes in hoarse voices as they shake the dice, but Diogenes and his fellow Christians prefer a quieter evening. He does not have to wait long for them, and when all are assembled he takes the roll of the Scriptures, a very precious possession, and reads to the little gathering. He recalls the deeds of their forefathers in the faith, of the old Israel, searching not only in what they said but also in what they did for prophecy of the Christ which was to come and His Church. At last his eyes begin to feel heavy with sleep, but before dismissing his guests he leads them in prayer:

> We praise Thee, we sing hymns to Thee, we bless Thee for Thy great glory, O Lord our King, the Father of Christ, the immaculate Lamb, who taketh away the sin of the world. Praise becomes Thee, glory becomes Thee, the God and Father, through the Son, in the most Holy Spirit, forever and ever. Amen.

It is time for bed and once again Diogenes lifts his heart and soul to God in prayer, thanking Him for the day he has spent, asking for His protection throughout the night, repeating the Lord's Prayer, and praising Him in the words of the Psalms:

> O sing unto the Lord a new song:
> let the congregation of saints praise him.
> Let the saints be joyful with glory:
> let them rejoice in their beds.

And so, as he makes the sign of the cross on his forehead and over his heart, his mind filled with the thought of his Lord and of His second coming to judge the world, Diogenes's day comes to a close.

There are a number of obvious omissions in the foregoing account. In the first place nothing is said of Diogenes's character, but to attempt any such delineation would be to desert the path of accurate factual description for that of fiction, since even the fresco can supply no clue, it being unlikely that it was intended to be a portrait. The nature of his work however enables one to conclude that he was intelligent and highly skilled, for he was in charge of a work of considerable magnitude, being himself not just a manual laborer, but also something of a miner, an engineer, an architect and an engraver, capable of executing all the manifold tasks which have been described.

In the second place, no attempt has so far been made to define his attitude to his work. As a member of an ancient and honorable corporation, whose importance was recognized by the Emperor Constantine himself,[27] *and as one who was numbered among the ranks of the clergy, belonging indeed to one of the seven orders of the inferior hierarchy, Diogenes doubtless took a justifiable pride in his profession, especially as the office of*

27 Constantine provided special habitations (*officinas*) for the sextons.

sexton was held to be consecrated in a sense by the visit of Christ to Lazarus's tomb. Was he not employed in burying the dead after the manner of holy Tobit? Was he not laboring, just as the Apostles did? Nor indeed would the fact that it was a menial task have detracted from its honor, for among Christians in Diogenes's day the distinctions of worldly rank were abolished, and as the Apostolic Constitutions *affirm: "Certainly he is a happy man who is able to support himself." Yet the sexton's gratification in his labor must have been tempered by a feeling of regret at the decreasing calls upon his services, for after the Peace of the Church open-air cemeteries became popular,*[28] *and at the time when Diogenes was in charge of Domitilla at least a third of the faithful were buried above ground, and this proportion was steadily increasing.*

The sexton's conception of the nature of his work has been happily preserved in an inscription which although partly mutilated has been ingeniously restored by de Rossi.[29] *The epitaph, which is in hexameters, is in the form of an imaginary dialogue between the sexton Innocentius, whose tomb it is, and the reader; in the course of the conversation Innocentius refers to his work, consisting of providing resting places for the people, as an act of prayer. The sextons therefore looked upon their duties not only as a vocation from*

[28] They had indeed been already in use in North Africa.
[29] *Roma sotteranea,* 1877, III, p. 543.

God, but as a continual offering of their toil and energies to Him. It has already been seen how much of their daily life was impregnated with the spirit of prayer, even such a simple act as the lighting of a lamp had a religious significance, and it is in keeping with this attitude, that they believed their labors to be an act of worship. The sextons were faithful to the teaching of St. Paul:

> *Whatsoever ye do, work heartily, as unto the Lord, and not unto men; knowing that from the Lord ye shall receive the recompense of the inheritance . . . for none of us liveth to himself. . . . For whether we live, we live unto the Lord; or whether we die, we die unto the Lord: whether we live therefore, or die, we are the Lord's.*[30]

[30] Col. 3: 23–24; Rom. 14: 7, 8.

5

John, A Bishop of Constantinople

A.D. 400

JOHN was born at Antioch about A.D. 345. His father, Secundus, held the important position of magister militiae, *but died while his son was still an infant, leaving the child's upbringing to his mother Anthusa, whose care and devotion can be compared only with that of Monica, the mother of Augustine. At the age of twenty-five John was baptized and shortly afterwards withdrew from Antioch to live the life of a hermit. He returned in 381 and was made a deacon and later ordained priest, and for seventeen years exercised his ministry in his home town, enthralling the populace with his virile and eloquent sermons. In 398 he was consecrated Bishop of Constantinople,*[1] *much against his will, and the peace he had previously enjoyed was*

[1] The title "patriarch" was introduced into the Church from the later organization of the Jews. While given to the bishops of Alexandria, Antioch, Constantinople, Jerusalem and Rome, in extraconciliar literature from the sixth century, it does not occur in the canons of the councils of the first eight centuries, and was not confined exclusively to these bishops until the ninth century.

soon shattered by the intrigues of which he found himself the object. His reforming zeal raised up against him a host of enemies, and, when they were joined by the Empress Eudoxia and led by that "weathercock" Theophilus of Alexandria, John found himself, despite the loyalty of his flock, incapable of defeating their unscrupulous designs. In June 404 he was exiled to Cucusus, a lonely village in the Taurus mountains, on the borders of Cilicia. Although vigorous efforts both in East and West to have him recalled were in vain, the time passed not unpleasantly for him, as he was visited by many of his devoted friends and occupied himself with the spiritual welfare of those amongst whom he was now compelled to live. In June 407 his enemies at court, incensed by the continued growth of his popularity and influence, arranged for his transference to Pityus, at the far eastern end of the Black Sea. The journey took three months and during the course of it John was subjected to the most harsh and cruel treatment, as a consequence of which he died on September 14 of the same year. In A.D. 438 his mortal remains were carried back to Constantinople, the Emperor Theodosius II, a son of Eudoxia, going in penitence to meet the cortege and praying the martyred bishop to intercede with God on behalf of his parents.

John's voluminous works consist almost entirely of sermons, delivered both at Antioch and Constantinople; it was these homilies, mainly in the form of commentaries on the books of the Bible, which earned for him the title of Chrysostom, Golden Mouth.

"If you only knew that a bishop is bound to belong to all, to bear the burden of all; that others, if they are angry, are pardoned, but he never; that others, if they sin, have excuses made for them, he has none; you would not be eager for the dignity, would not run after it. So it is, the bishop is exposed to the tongues of all, to the criticism of all whether they be wise or fools. He is harassed with cares every day, indeed every night. He has many to hate him, many to envy him. Then, again, if he does not give to all, the idle and the industrious alike, see! A thousand complaints on all sides. No one is afraid to accuse him and speak evil of him. Why speak of the anxiety connected with the ministry of the word and with doctrine? The painful work in ordinations? Either I am a poor wretched incompetent creature, or else the case is as I say. The soul of the bishop is for all the world like a vessel in a storm, lashed from every side, by friends, by foes, by one's own people, by strangers. I do not think there are many among bishops that will be saved, but many more that perish: and the reason is that it is an affair that requires a great mind. Many are the exigencies which throw a man out of his natural temper, and he needs to have a thousand eyes on all sides. Do you not see what a number of qualifications a bishop must have? To be apt to teach, patient, holding fast the faithful word in doctrine. What trouble and pains does this require! And then others do wrong and he bears all the blame! Let him be angry, let him laugh, or let him but dream of a moment's relaxation, there are many to scoff, many to be offended, many to lay down the law, many to bring to mind the former bishops and abuse the present one; not that they wish to sound the praise of those — no, it is only to carp at him that they bring up the mention of fellow bishops. In short, the bishop is distracted on every side, and is expected to do many things that are beyond his power. If he does not know how to speak, there is great murmuring; and if he can speak, then he is accused of pride. If he cannot raise the dead, he is worthless, they say; such a one is pious, but this man is not. If he eats a moderate meal, for this he is accused, he ought to be strangled, they say. In fine, he ought not to look upon the sun!" [2]

Though refreshed by his sleep, it is thoughts such as these, thoughts which he originally expressed while still a presbyter at Antioch and which he has now proved sadly true in his own experience as Bishop of Constantinople, that weigh heavily on John as he rises from his bed. But the miniature Gospel book hanging by his bed [3] and the painting of the flying sickle of

[2] *In Act. hom.*, iii; *in Tit. hom.*, i.

[3] This practice probably underlies the traditional verse:

Matthew, Mark, Luke and John
Bless the bed that I lie on.

judgment above it[4] are symbols of that faith which enables him to bear the burden of episcopal authority with a steady determination to seek God's will in all things.

> O God, thou art my God; early will I seek thee:
> My soul thirsteth for thee, my flesh longeth for thee,
> In a dry and weary land where no water is.

It is with the words of the Sixty-third Psalm that John begins his morning prayer.

> My mouth shall praise thee with joyful lips;
> When I remember thee upon my bed,
> And meditate upon thee in the night watches.
>
> My soul followeth hard after thee:
> Thy right hand upholdeth me.
> But those that seek my soul, to destroy it,
> Shall go into the lower parts of the earth.

John continues with a favorite and habitual prayer which he first heard in his early youth from an old monk:

> I give thanks to Thee, Heavenly Father, for all Thy benefits shewn forth upon me, the unworthy, from the first day until the present, for what I know, and what I do not know, for the seen, for the unseen, for those in deed, those in word, those with my will, those against my will, for all that has been bestowed upon

[4] The reference is to the LXX of Zech. 5: 1–3.

> the unworthy, even me; for tribulations, for refreshments, for hell, for punishments, for the kingdom of heaven. I beseech Thee to keep my soul holy, having a pure conscience; an end worthy of Thy loving kindness. Thou that lovest me so as to give Thine Only-begotten Son for me, grant me to become worthy of Thy love; give me wisdom in Thy word, and in Thy fear, Only-begotten Christ, inspire the strength that is from Thee. Thou that gavest Thine Only-begotten Son for me, and hast sent Thy Holy Spirit for the remission of my sins, if in anything I have willfully or unwittingly transgressed, pardon and impute it not; remember all that call upon Thy name in truth; remember all that wish me well, or the contrary, for we are all men.

Then the bishop sums up his aspirations in the prayer of the faithful, the Lord's Prayer.

Crossing to a little basin on a table by the window, John rinses his hands as a mark of reverence before reading the Scriptures, and, taking a codex from a wall bookcase, he settles down on a chair to study and meditate. This is the most peaceful time of his day, before the uproar of the streets bursts through the windows, before the continual stream of callers, before the incessant demands of administrative and spiritual duties have to be answered. To John it is like leaving the noise and bustle of the town for a quiet meadow, strewn with flowers heavy with an abundant fragrance, and not only a meadow but even a paradise, for the flowers bear fruit capable of nourishing the soul. The moments of refreshment pass quickly and by half past eight John has to lay aside his book and dress himself for the celebration of the Eucharist. He has no special vestments, just his ordinary outdoor wear, which consists of a *tunica alba*, a white garment reaching to the ground with long sleeves, a *paenula*, a semicircular piece of material fastened down the center front with an opening for the head, and around his neck an *orarium*, a small towel with which he can wipe his hands or his mouth.[5]

Shortly before nine o'clock John leaves his palace; he is a familiar figure with his pale hollow cheeks, his long beard and deep-sunken eyes, his ample but wrinkled forehead and his bald head, and as he skirts the north side of the Augusteum on his way to the entrance of Sancta Sophia, erected by the Emperor Constantius some forty years before,[6] he acknowledges many greetings. The steps leading up to the great gate of the church are thronged with beggars, eagerly accepting alms from the faithful who are passing into the colonnaded atrium. Washing their hands in the fountain which occupies the center of the forecourt, the

5 From these three the later alb, chasuble and stole developed.

6 Possibly Constantine the Great laid the foundations. The first church was burned down in 404, restored by Theodosius II and rededicated in 415; burned again in the Nika sedition of 532, rebuilt by Justinian and rededicated in 537. This Justinian church is the present building, with some alterations and additions, and is now a Byzantine museum after being for centuries a Turkish mosque.

men and women mount the steps and enter through separate doors under the supervision of the deacons. It is with some irritation that John notices the way in which several of his flock stoop and kiss the porch, others touching it with their hands and then putting them to their mouths; he has little time for these practices which betray minds still subservient to pagan superstitions.

The archdeacon Serapion is awaiting the bishop and accompanies him into the nave as soon as the presbyters have collected. Advancing to the sanctuary, John and his assistants mount the steps; taking his place in front of his throne, with the presbyters standing in a semicircle about him, the deacons on either side of the altar, the bishop faces the congregation across the holy table and greets them with the words:

"Peace be with you."

"And with thy spirit," answers the assembly in one voice.

The first part of the service, the synaxis, or Mass of the catechumens, now continues with readings from the Old Testament, the Epistles and the Gospels, chants dividing one from the other. The sermon is to follow and John makes his way to the ambon or lectern in the nave; for, although the usual custom is for the bishop to address the faithful from his throne, John's asceticism during his life as a hermit has so impaired his health, his gastric organs and kidneys having been affected, that he often remarks jokingly that he has a cobweb body and his voice is too frail to carry to all corners of the large building.

Each section of the community has its own appointed place, the lesser orders of the ministry in the body of the church, the men in the side aisles, and above them in the tribunes or galleries the women, with the virgins and widows in the position of honor.[7] Today there is silent expectancy as they await the text, for the numbers are less than those who attend the Sunday service, when there is a tumult of noise, a confused hubbub of laughter, and the distraction is so great that it is difficult not to imagine oneself in the public baths or in a wine shop. The duties of religion have become for many formalities only fullfilled to relieve the conscience; it is a matter of routine. It is almost impossible to distinguish the conduct here on those occasions from that in the market or on the stage, for pickpockets are plying their trade, scandalmongers are gossiping of this and that, there is talk of politics, of the army, of buying and selling. Many of the women are decked in all their finery, "mouth like a bear's mouth dyed with blood, eyebrows blackened as with the smut of a kitchen utensil, cheeks whitened with dust like the walls of a tomb"; so that many profligates who desire to corrupt a woman think no place is more suit-

[7] There were, however, probably no galleries in the first church of Sancta Sophia, galleries being a later Eastern feature; hence women would occupy one of the side aisles.

able than the church. On this Monday morning, however, when only the devout find the time and have the inclination to be present, the conduct is more seemly, more befitting the sacred precincts which are to John a place of angels, a place of archangels, a temple of God — heaven itself.

"AND BEHOLD, ONE CAME AND SAID UNTO HIM, GOOD MASTER, BY DOING WHAT SHALL I INHERIT ETERNAL LIFE?" [8]

John leans forward in the pulpit, the more to command the ready attention of those standing or sitting before him.[9]

> Some indeed accuse this young man, as one dissembling and ill-minded, and coming with a temptation to Jesus, but I would by no means call him a dissembler, since Mark says: "Jesus beheld him, and loved him."
>
> But the tyranny of wealth is very great and although we be virtuous about all other things, this ruins everything; "the love of money is the root of all evils."

The bishop's voice is pleasant to listen to, plain and natural, distinct in pronunciation, free from any twang or theatrical accent.[10]

8 Chrysostom, *Comm. in Mtt. Hom.*, lxiii. Although preached at Antioch, not Constantinople, and although not the most sparkling of his efforts, this abbreviated sermon is given here as a basis for comparison with Clement of Alexandria's treatment of the same text.

9 There were few pews in the early churches; some wooden ones were provided for the aged in the side aisles, and the chancels linking the bases of the pillars were often used for seating, but the whole center nave remained free.

10 Cf. the strictures of St. Ambrose on the "parson's voice": "The voice should not be languid, nor feeble, nor womanish in tone — such

Now what does Christ say in reply to the young man's earnest desire? "If thou wilt be perfect, go and sell that thou hast, and give to the poor, and thou shalt have treasure in heaven, and come, follow me. But when the young man heard it, he went away sorrowful" and Christ said "How hardly shall the rich enter into the kingdom of heaven!" blaming not riches, but those who are held in subjection by them. But if the rich man "hardly," much more the covetous man. For if not to give one's own be a hindrance to entering the kingdom, even to take of other men's goods, think how much fire it heaps up!

But how may this very thing be done, you may say, to forsake these? How is it possible for him that is once sunk in such lust of wealth to recover himself? If he begin to empty himself of his possessions, and cut off what are superfluous. For so shall he both advance further, and shall run on his course more easily afterwards.

Through the translucent marble plates covering the window openings a shaft of sunlight falls directly on John's head, giving him an angelic appearance as he warms to his subject.

Do not then seek all at once, but gently ascend the ladder that leads you up to heaven. For just as those in a fever having a profusion of acrid bile inside them, when they shovel in on top of it meats and drinks, so far from quenching their thirst, just kindle the flame;

a tone of voice as many are in the habit of using, under the idea of seeming important." (*De officiis ministrorum,* I, 84.)

so also the covetous when they shovel in their wealth upon this wicked lust more acrid than bile, do rather inflame it. For nothing so stays it as to refrain for a time from the lust of gain, just as acrid bile is stayed by abstinence and evacuations. But how can this be done?

At this rhetorical question John pauses and looks solemnly round the church.

How can this be done? If you consider that as long as you are rich you will never cease thirsting and pining with the lust for more; but being freed from your possessions you will be able to stay this disease. Do not then surround yourself with more, in case you strive for things unattainable, and be incurable and more miserable than all, being thus frantic.

Therefore that we may not have superfluous sorrows, let us forsake the love of money that is ever paining and never endures to hold its peace, and let us remove ourselves to another love, which both makes us happy and has great felicity, and let us long after the treasures above. Considering all these things, put away the wicked desire of wealth.

But seeing perhaps the brightness of the silver, and the multitude of servants, and the beauty of the buildings, the court paid in the market place, are you bewitched by it? What remedy then may there be for this evil wound? If you consider how these things affect the soul, how dark and desolate and foul they render it, and how ugly; if you reckon with how many evils these things were acquired, with how many labors they are kept.

A look of concern appears on the faces of the listeners at the thought of this inward corruption. John continues:

> When then you see anyone resplendent outwardly with raiment and large attendance, lay open his conscience, and you shall see many a cobweb within and more dust. Consider the Son of God Himself, who hath not where to lay His head. Be an imitator of Him, and of His servants, and imagine to yourself the unspeakable riches of these.
>
> So let us emulate the things worthy of emulation, not gorgeous buildings, not costly estates, but the men that have much confidence towards God, those that have riches in heaven, the owners of those treasures, them that are really rich, them that are poor for Christ's sake, that we may attain unto the good things of eternity by the grace and love towards man of our Lord Jesus Christ, with whom be unto the Father, together with the Holy Spirit, glory, might, honor, now and always and world without end. Amen.

Despite John's many protests against the practice, the applause which follows the end of this exhortation is loud and long, and it is several minutes before the deacon is able to offer up the prayer for the catechumens,[11] those candidates for baptism who are stand-

[11] In many churches those undergoing public penance also had their place in the porch and were dismissed at this point in the service, but this practice seems to have been discontinued at Constantinople at the end of the fourth century. (Sozomen, *Historia ecclesiastica,* vii. 16.)

ing in the porch of the church [12] and who are now dismissed with the bishop's blessing. Unlike the Sunday when many of the faithful themselves leave after the sermon, with the lame excuse that they can pray equally well at home, only a few take the opportunity of withdrawing with the catechumens. The deacons then close and lock the doors of the church, drawing a golden curtain across them, for only those who have been incorporated into the Body of Christ by baptism may join in making the solemn offering.

Intercessions follow, for the world, for the Catholic Church, for peace, for those in distress. Then John salutes the congregation: "The peace of the Lord be always with you"; and the Kiss of Peace is exchanged: the bishop with the clergy around his throne, the women with the women, and the men with the men — a token of that love which the Holy Spirit, the bond of unity and peace, sheds abroad in the hearts of the faithful.

While the bishop is rinsing his hands from a ewer and wiping them on his *orarium*, the deacons go to a table in one of the side aisles to collect the people's offerings, which they have already received and prepared before the service began. The gifts are carried

12 This was the Western custom; in the East the porch was incorporated into the body of the church, being known as the narthex; but although common in Greece in the fourth century it was not universal in the East until the sixth, and it is reasonable to suppose that it was not a part of the first church of Sancta Sophia.

to the sanctuary and presented to the bishop and his presbyters, who have moved forward from their seats to take their place immediately behind the altar facing the congregation.[13]

"The Lord be with you."

"And with thy spirit."

"Lift up your hearts."

"We lift them up unto the Lord."

The angels' song follows, when, to John at least, the worship on earth joins with that in heaven; then the recitation of the words of institution and the invocation of the Holy Spirit to descend upon the elements. There is complete silence now, even the air is still, apart from the gentle motion of the fans wafted by the deacons to banish the flies, for Christ Himself is present, the awe-inspiring table is spread before them bearing the Lamb of God. Serapion, the archdeacon, takes the list of the faithful departed and reads aloud the names of those bishops who have preceded John in the see and of those emperors who have served the cause of

[13] A difference is to be noted here between the Western practice at the offertory when the people themselves brought their gifts to the altar, and the fourth-century Syrian usage which involved the presentation of the gifts before the service and their being brought up at the offertory by the deacons alone. This latter custom eventually spread all over the Middle East, and was certainly known to Chrysostom while he was at Antioch. Whether or not it had actually been adopted at Constantinople by the year 400, as stated above, it is difficult to say — it is possible. It is equally possible that Chrysostom himself was responsible for the change since the ascription of a liturgy to him, albeit in its present form a liturgy dating from the sixth or seventh centuries, may suggest some innovations by him.

Christ.[14] After the Lord's Prayer, John breaks the bread for distribution, the presbyters, who are concelebrating, performing the same actions.[15]

"Holy things to the holy," proclaims John, raising the paten; then he communicates, followed by the presbyters and deacons. The people advance reverently to the chancel rail, going first to the one who is administering the bread with the words "The Body of Christ," to which they reply "Amen," then moving to Serapion for the chalice: "The Blood of Christ," "Amen." They receive standing. Since the end of the Communion marks the real termination of the rite, the ablutions are next taken, the holy vessels being cleansed, and then after a brief thanksgiving one of the deacons dismisses the assembly with the words: "Depart in peace." Most of them immediately make their way out into the porticoes of the atrium, to John's regret, for he would like them to imitate his example of staying some little time for recollection and meditation.

As he emerges into the forecourt, John is greeted by one of the faithful, a rich and prominent citizen, who stoops and kisses his hand. They engage in conversation and the bishop broaches a subject which is near to his heart; he is anxious to provide churches for the many

14 Diptychs (lists of the dead and living) were not introduced at Constantinople until a few years later.

15 That is, they have bread on patens held by the deacons and perform the same manual acts as the bishop, who alone says the eucharistic prayer.

country districts which are without them, and he suggests that the rich man might with advantage employ some of his wealth in the erecting of a church in the vicinity of his country estate.

"The outlay would be more than I can afford at the moment, holy father."

"Then why not join with some of your friends, or alternatively, build the church in sections — start with the sanctuary and then add to it as you are able; or leave it to your heirs, one could build a porch, another an atrium, and so on." [16]

"It is a matter which requires careful consideration, your honor and dignity."

"Quite, but it would certainly benefit the village; think how it would foster community life; the friendships formed there by people would not be struck up at random nor promiscuously, and the meetings there would be far more pleasant than those which take place in markets and fairs."

"I agree; I will certainly look into it."

John turns to talk to others of his flock when his attention is arrested by a child who is wearing a strand of red wool around her arm, and accompanying her is a little boy with a medallion hanging from his neck bearing the likeness of Alexander. These superstitions annoy him intensely, and there are so many of them.

16 This surprisingly modern expedient is suggested by Chrysostom in his commentary on Acts, *Hom.*, xviii.

There is the custom of collecting mud from the bottom of the baths and smearing the forehead with it to avert evil and jealousy; there is the tying of the names of rivers around children to ward off diseases, or the placing of a copy of the Gospel on the head to cure fever; and as for the choice of names, instead of using those of a saint and a martyr, which would be most fit and proper, they give the children heathen names, which at the birth they mark on candles so that they may accept the one which burns the longest. This red wool is evidence of the same attitude of mind, and it is supposed to turn away the evil eye, witchcraft and envy. John goes up to the mother and in no uncertain terms orders the offending strand to be taken off and the medallion to be replaced by a simple cross.

"By Christ," says the father, who is standing nearby, "these are harmless enough practices, but if your honor and dignity wishes it, they shall be removed."

"Are you aware," asks John in some heat, "that I have asked the sacristans to report to me any that they hear swearing so that I may excommunicate them? Parrots are known because they speak like men. Christians should be known by speaking like angels; let this be a mark to distinguish us from the heathen amongst whom we live. Let your oath be an imprecation upon your own child, upon your own self: say, 'Else let the hangman lash my ribs.' But you dare not. Is God less valuable than your ribs? Is He less precious than your pate? Say, 'Else let me be struck blind.' But no, Christ so spares us that He will not even let us swear by our own head, and yet we so little spare the honor of God, that on all occasions we must drag Him in! That precious Name which is above every name, the Name which is marvelous in all the earth, the Name which devils hear and tremble. We hiss about as we like! Oh, the force of habit! It is by this means the Name has become cheap. I will not exercise my authority on this occasion, as it may be you have not heard my warning, but should you indulge in this pernicious practice any further I shall have no hesitation in excommunicating you immediately."

John turns on his heel and, accompanied by Serapion, leaves the atrium and crosses the Augusteum to his palace.

"You know, Serapion," says the bishop, as they go into his study, "I cannot bear to ascend this throne without effecting some great reformation. If this be impossible, it is better to stand below. There is nothing more wretched than a ruler who does his people no good."

"You will never subdue these mutinous priests until you drive them before you with a rod."

"Our severity must be tempered with wisdom," replies John, tapping the palm of his left hand with the forefinger of his right, a familiar gesture when he is deep in thought. "Moreover the issues are not always clear-cut; for example, how would you deal with a clerk who ought never to have been ordained?"

"Cut him off."

"You cannot do that because he is not guilty of any present fault, yet if you do not call him to account for the past, on the grounds that the bishop who ordained him is answerable, the time will come when he is ripe for promotion and to refuse to allow it would be to punish his unworthiness, and call attention to the scandal of his being ordained in the first instance; to advance him would be even worse. No, Serapion, the situation is more complex than you are prepared to allow."

"There is one matter, your honor and dignity, where you can act with firmness and that is over the question of these housekeepers."

"Yes, this practice of the clergy keeping women in their houses, some of them very young, some of them even under vows of virginity, gives rise to great temptation. They are worse than brothel-keepers, these men, and what is more, the holy fathers at Nicaea expressly forbade the introduction of any women into the house except a mother, a sister or an aunt. One of the presbyters attached to the Church of the Holy Apostles is particularly blameworthy in this respect and I intend to call on him this afternoon and try to make him see the scandal of his position. But the presbyters are not the only ones whose conduct is reprehensible; have you seen the charges brought against the Bishop of Ephesus?"

"I have only heard of them."

"They have been formulated under seven heads by Eusebius, Bishop of Valentinopolis. He charges Antoninus in the first place with having melted down church plate and placed the proceeds to the account of his son; second, that he has set up pillars belonging to the Church, which had been in position for many years, in his own dining room; next, that he has removed marble from the entrance to the baptistery and used it for the improvement of his own bathroom; fourth, that his servant has committed murder, and that he is still keeping him in his service without bringing him to trial; fifth, that he has sold some land bequeathed to the Church by Basilina, the mother of the Emperor Julian, and has kept the money; sixth, that after separating from his wife [17] he has taken her again and has had children by her; finally, that he regards it as a law to sell consecrations to bishoprics at prices in proportion to the emoluments. If Eusebius can produce proof of these accusations, then it is a very serious

[17] Bishops and presbyters were not allowed to marry after ordination, but if they were married beforehand it was the custom to allow cohabitation to continue. In time the West disallowed this for both bishop and presbyter, while the East only ordered the separation of a bishop from his wife, permitting a presbyter to remain in the married state.

matter and I shall probably have to go to Ephesus to look into it."[18]

Further deliberation is brought to an end by the entrance of Domitian, the steward, who has been summoned by John to go through the church accounts, and for the next hour the three of them are busy examining the books and considering questions of expenditure.

The Church's revenues are derived from many sources. There are the freewill offerings of the faithful, in the form of daily, weekly and monthly oblations. There are the various lands and property which, under a law of Constantine, it is now possible to bequeath to the Church; added to these there are the estates of the martyrs and of any clergy dying intestate. A regular allowance is also made from the imperial exchequer, and the collection of tithes and first fruits provides altogether a very considerable income. But on the debit side there are many demands to be met. The Christians at Constantinople number some hundred thousand and they hold themselves responsible for the maintenance of fifty thousand poor folk, to which may be added a further three thousand widows and virgins who depend upon the Church for their means of subsistence. To their support a quarter of the income is devoted, the remaining three quarters being required for the bishop,

[18] Chrysostom had indeed to go to Ephesus and his absence together with the disciplinary measures he took contributed materially to his eventual exile.

for the stipends of the clergy and for the upkeep of the churches, their fabric, lights, and other necessities.

John is anxious that the finances should be managed with scrupulous honesty and refuses to benefit the Church at the expense of other deserving causes; he will not for example allow fathers to disinherit their children in favor of the Church, and on one occasion already has returned an estate which had been left out of the deceased's family. After careful consideration it is decided that certain grants which are of no benefit to the Church are to be discontinued; that John's own expenditure on hospitality and food shall be drastically curtailed, the money so saved being used for the hospital; and that his own income should be decreased in favor of the poor-fund. Although the task is a necessary one, John finds it irksome.

"Nowadays," he says, as the final column is checked, "my fellow bishops have gone beyond agents and hucksters in their care about these things, and when they ought to be careful and thoughtful about your souls they are vexing themselves every day about financial matters, for which the innkeepers and taxgatherers and accountants are careful.[19] However, I think everything now is more or less in order and I leave it to you, Domitian, to see that it is kept so. There is one further

[19] Originally Church revenues were entrusted entirely to the bishop, who was assisted by the archdeacon; by Chrysostom's day the appointing of a steward had become usual, thus relieving the bishop of the need for continual concern about financial matters.

point: will you see that the recipients of any charity are told the names of their individual benefactors in order that they may pray for them?"

In one of the large rooms of the episcopal palace a number of people is gathering, for it is nearly half past eleven, the time when the bishop sits in judgment on those secular and civil cases which are referred to him in accordance with St. Paul's injunction that the faithful are not to go to law before unbelievers.[20] These hearings always take place on a Monday in order that, should any controversy arise about the decision, it may be settled before the following Sunday and the parties be set at peace with one another.

John takes his place with his presbyters and deacons, and the preliminary investigation of the characters of the plaintiff and the defendant begins. Is this the first person the plaintiff has accused or has he advanced accusations against others before? Does the accusation arise from a personal quarrel, independent of the rights and wrongs of the case? What manner of life has he led hitherto? Turning to the defendant, John inquires as to his mode of life also; whether he has been unblamable; whether he has been notable for his piety; whether he has a regard for the order of widows; whether he has a love of strangers, a love of the poor, and a love of the brethren; whether he is not given to filthy lucre; whether he be not an extravagant person

[20] Episcopal jurisdiction had also received state recognition.

or a spendthrift; whether he be sober and free from luxury or a drunkard and a glutton; whether he be compassionate and charitable. Having satisfied himself on these points, the bishop asks both parties to stand in the middle of the court and make their speeches.

"Holy father," the plaintiff begins, "my brother, who is a bishop of the Church, has granted one of our family estates to our widowed sister on the condition that it should pass at her death to the Church. Now my brother is a decurion and it is forbidden by the law for one in such a position to sell or alienate in any way his goods and property without the authorization of the prefect, since his hereditary membership of the *curia* involves heavy expenses which must be met. As I am his legal heir and shall succeed him in this office, with the consequent necessity to defray the expenses incurred in its exercise, I have applied in the prefect's court to have this agreement annulled. Since no settlement has so far been reached, I am appealing to you to give judgment in this matter."

"Your honor and dignity," the accused makes his defense, "it is true that I am a decurion and that my brother is my legal heir and will succeed me in that office, but by a law of the year 361 the august Emperor Constantius enacted that all clergy who were decurions should forfeit their material possessions upon ordination with the exception of those consecrated to the episcopacy. As a bishop, under this law, I retain full rights over my patrimony, and my brother has no grounds for objecting to this agreement with my sister."

"I protest" says the plaintiff, "that my grounds for objection are entirely valid. I admit that by the law of Constantius you are permitted to retain your property, and I am not asking for it to be given to me, but the law does not state that you have any right to dispose of it in such a way that it ceases to be available for the charges of the *curia.* Under this law you have no right to give part of the family inheritance to one who has no legal responsibility to defray the expenses of the *curia,* nor to affirm that it must eventually be bestowed upon the Church. Moreover, this same law, which you quote, explicitly states that a decurion who becomes a cleric in the lower orders of the ministry must give his fortune to the nearest relative in the line of succession; I contend that by analogy a bishop should preserve his patrimony that it may descend eventually intact to his heir."

John listens to argument and counterargument; witnesses are called, since according to Scripture each statement must be established at the mouth of two or three witnesses; then, after deliberation with his presbyters and deacons, he gives his judgment:

"I direct that the land in question shall be given to the brother who is the legal heir; that he shall be given this property on the condition of an annual payment in corn, wine and oil to his sister; that, after her decease, he shall retain possession of the estate without obligation to further payment either to his brother, or to the Church. I trust that this decision will satisfy all parties, since the plaintiff will receive the land, his sister will have a fixed income for life guaranteed, and the defendant will have this unfortunate dissension in his family brought to an end. The only loser is the Church, but the Church is rich in things eternal and can afford to dispense with temporal gains." [21]

The session is declared closed, and John, accompanied by one of his deacons, goes to the door of his palace, where his mule is already waiting for him. Seating himself on the saddle, he urges the animal off at a walking pace round the Golden Milarium, a rectangular monument with vaulted arcades opening into its four sides which serves as the starting point for the measurement of the imperial roads. Turning to the left, past the baths of Zeuxippus, he guides the mule along a branch road towards the Strategion, for he is going to pay a visit to the prison.

[21] It must be admitted that the utilization of this case in the narrative is open to objection, since by a law of Arcadius in 399 even bishops were ordered either to find substitutes for the curia, endowing them with their property, or to resign their property entirely to the curia; hence this case, one originally brought before St. Ambrose in 378, could not have been heard in the year 400 as represented in the text. It has nevertheless been included, because (1) the hearing of civil cases was an important part of a bishop's work, and (2) this is one of the best documented cases to have been preserved (Ambrose, *Ep.*, lxxxii) and therefore is very suitable for detailed and accurate description. It is fully considered by F. Martroye, "*Une sentence arbitrale de Saint-Ambroise,*" *Revue Historique de Droit Français et Etranger,* 1929, pp. 300–311.

The state prison at Constantinople, as others throughout the empire, is not a large building, for it is nonresidential in the sense that it is only a place where the accused are lodged while their trial is pending; there are no sentences of imprisonment under the law, only enslavement, forced labor in the mines or death. Its inmates are therefore only birds of passage, but since the imperial exchequer is only chargeable for coarse bread and water, there is a great need for the exercise of Christian charity in the form of gifts in kind.

As John approaches the heavy iron gates he sees some of the prisoners, in their chains, returning from the market place, whither they have been sent by the jailers to beg; the bishop knows only too well the blows and curses they will receive if they have not been very successful. Dismounting, John passes the time of the day with the turnkey, to whom he is a familiar figure as a frequent visitor, then enters the first ward of the prison.[22] The scene is such as to touch the hardest heart; some are in bonds, others covered with filth, others have uncut hair and are clad in rags; many are almost wild with hunger, and come running to grovel at his feet like dogs snapping for food. John takes from the bag which the deacon has carried some of the bread and wine set aside at the Eucharist for this purpose, and takes care to see that each has something.

[22] Those in the inner ward, where Victoria was placed, were not allowed to have visitors.

His gifts are accompanied with sympathetic words; he appreciates their sadness and their humility, but urges them to let their affliction soften any harshness they may have and promote courage and endurance. With some he prays, to others he gives a word of advice, all find in him some moral sustenance and it is with genuine sorrow that they eventually see him depart.

In the main thoroughfare there is shouting and jostling, and John has to halt as the Emperor Arcadius sweeps by in proud procession to his palace overlooking the Hippodrome. His men are dressed in golden armor and even his pairs of white mules are proudly decked in gold; his chariots are set with jewels and furnished with snow-white cushions, spangles flutter about them and dragons are shaped out in silken hangings; the shields have golden bosses and their straps are studded with gems; there are gilded trappings for the horses, and their bits, too, are plated with gold; eunuchs, black-liveried servants, fan-bearers, all hurry past in sycophantic attendance upon Arcadius, who himself is seated high on a throne, resplendent in his purple robe and diadem.

Once they have gone by, John and his deacon continue their way to the forum of Constantine, with its double tier of porticoes, entering it by a lofty marble archway at one end of the ellipse. The crowd is so thick that it is almost impossible to move; around the hundred-and-twenty-foot porphyry column in the center which now bears a statue of Theodosius,[23] camels, mules and asses, jugglers, mountebanks and beggars are mingled together, pushing this way and that. Here a man is throwing up knives and catching them dexterously by the handles; there another is balancing a pole on his forehead while two children are wrestling on the top of it; trained swallows are settling on the nose of a third to take crumbs out of his mouth, while his companion is chewing nails and devouring shoes; beggars, whistling on pipes, have their fingers inserted in cups, bowls and cans, on which they are playing like cymbals. A tame lion is being paraded up and down, and around the specially anointed torsos of some men snakes are writhing and twining. A war dance is in progress, performed by the so-called "Titans" who, feigning madness, flourish their swords frantically and then wreak their artificial fury on a luckless cur who happens to be sneaking by. As the performers are rewarded by pieces of bread and halfpennies, they redouble their efforts and their noise, and John is thankful to emerge through the further archway into the comparative quietness of the street beyond. A little distance along and he turns into the side street where the hospital is to be found, the closeness of the buildings affording some shade and some relaxation to the eyes after the glaring sun in the forum.

23 At first there was a statue of Constantine, which was replaced by one of Julian.

The bishop and his deacon are greeted at the door by Nicarete, a well-to-do Bithynian lady of noble birth, whom John has frequently pressed to act as instructress to the virgins and who has as frequently refused, considering herself unworthy. She spends much of her time in the hospital, preparing a variety of remedies for the needs of the sick and having no little success in curing them. On his inquiry about one of the patients who has had a polypus in his nose, John is pleased to hear that as the result of a violent fit of coughing the noxious creature has been expelled, but he is sorry to learn that another who has a fever and obstinately refuses to gargle is suffering from a temporarily paralyzed tongue.

The sick are cared for in long wards with berths or divans running along the walls; the lepers are isolated in one section, and another room, its windows heavily shuttered, is set apart for those suffering from ophthalmia. The medical attendants are busy changing dressings as John enters; one patient with a great gash in his forearm is having the plaster removed before it is cleaned with corrosive powder — should it spread further, it will be seared and the putrid flesh excised, then fomentations and oil will be applied; another is having a gangrenous cut opened with a lancet, while a third is having a wound dilated with a small adjustable vice. The bishop is pleased to see some of the widows there helping with the menial tasks, gently washing away the matter discharged from wounds, moistening the lips of those too old to move and helping the cripples to eat.

At the farther end of the ward the doctor is explaining the rudiments of medical science to a student:

"This body of ours consists of four elements, namely, of what is warm, that is, of blood; of what is dry, that is, of yellow bile; of what is moist, that is, of phlegm; of what is cold, that is, of black bile. The health of the body depends upon a right balance of these elements, disturbance of it produces illness and if it is not counteracted death ensues. So, for example, excess of yellow bile leads to fever." [24]

He discontinues his instruction upon seeing the bishop and comes to pay his respects and at the same time to ask John if he will anoint certain of his patients. The bishop is quite prepared for this request and, going to a young woman's bed, he prays for her restoration to health. Taking a flask from his deacon, he dips his fingers into the oil, which has been blessed at the previous Sunday Eucharist, and applies this *oleum infirmorum* to the affected parts, to the head and the breast, at the same time beseeching God that every fever and every demon and every sickness may depart

[24] It is probable that the doctor would derive most of his ideas from Oribasius (A.D. 325–403), who was physician in ordinary to the Emperor Julian and sometime quaestor of Constantinople; but the theories of Oribasius were in the main a reproduction of those of Galen, who, although far more original, drew numerous elements, including the theory outlined above, from Hippocrates via Aristotle.

through this unction and that the young woman may be strengthened and sanctified.[25]

By the time John has anointed the other patients and made his rounds of the several wards, the afternoon is well advanced, and mounting his mule once again he turns its head in the direction of the Church of the Holy Apostles. As he turns aside to avoid a litter on which is being carried the obese figure of a gluttonous fellow, swathed in bandages because of gout, his belly distended like that of a woman with child, the bishop's attention is drawn to a girl whom a man is forcibly hustling along, obviously against her will. Recognizing that they are both Christians, John calls to them and asks what they are about.

"I have a lawsuit, holy father," replies the man, "and I am taking this girl to a synagogue to swear an oath that she will be a faithful witness."

"I have refused and I still refuse to take an oath in front of Jews."

"Swearing is expressly forbidden by Our Lord," remonstrates John. "He says, 'Swear not at all; neither by the heaven, for it is the throne of God; nor by the earth, for it is the footstool of his feet; nor by Jerusalem, for it is the city of the great King. Neither shalt thou swear by the head, for thou canst not make one hair

[25] This practice was widespread in the early Church, having Scriptural precedent in Jas. 5: 14, 15; it was quite common even when the person anointed was in no danger of death. In this lies the origin of Extreme Unction.

white or black; but let your yea be yea, and your nay, nay.' And further, the use of force to make someone swear against their will is even more reprehensible. So I forbid you to continue with this on the pain of excommunication. But why, I fail to understand, do you choose a synagogue for this?"

"I have been assured that oaths made in a synagogue are more powerful than others."

John's immediate reaction is one of indignation, but the absurdity of the idea is so patent that his further remonstrances give way to laughter and, having received assurances from the man that he will do no more about it, he pursues his way in a good humor.[26]

The house of the offending presbyter whose conduct John has discussed with Serapion during the course of the morning is near the Church of the Holy Apostles, a magnificent cruciform building, its bronze tiles gleaming in the sun, which enshrines the stone sarcophagus of the Emperor Constantine. Crosses are inscribed on the door and windows, and John makes the same sign as he enters, being admitted by the same young woman who is the cause of his visit. His interview with the presbyter is conducted with delicacy and tact,[27] and he

[26] Chrysostom had a whimsical sense of humor which expressed itself in the giving of nicknames denoting the opposite of the person's character; thus he would call a sober man a drunkard, and so on.

[27] It is often said by historians that Chrysostom was overbearing and peremptory in his dealings with offenders, but his account of how to manage such a case as that described above, given in his forty-fourth homily on 1 Corinthians, is a model of diplomacy.

begins by praising him for those virtues which he is known to possess, fomenting him with his commendations, as it were with warm water, so mitigating the tumor of his wound.

"For myself, I must confess that I am wretched; I share with you a sinful nature and I feel I must ask your pardon for undertaking things which are too great for me, but yet charity persuades me to dare all things."

John gives his advice not imperiously but in a brotherly fashion, pointing out that the keeping of a young unmarried woman in his house is bound to give rise to scandal as well as laying himself open to a temptation which, under the circumstances, it is hard to resist.

"This proceeding considered in itself is hardly a matter for praise, for it is not commendable to keep house with a woman who is a virgin. I know indeed that you do it for God's sake, and that the unprotected state of this poor woman affected you and caused you to take this step. I am not saying these things to direct but to remind you. But let us see whether another evil is not produced by it. If there be none, keep her in your house and stick to this excellent purpose. There is no one to hinder you. But if any mischief arises from it exceeding the advantage, let us take care, I beg of you, lest while we are earnest to comfort one soul, we put a stumbling-block in the way of ten thousand. You have no need to learn these things of me; you yourself know if any offend one of these little ones how great a penalty is threatened."

"But what of her position, holy father? She has no one to turn to."

"Let none of these considerations disturb you; you will have ample excuse, namely the offense given to others, since not in indifference but for care towards them you will have expelled her. So I advise you to discontinue the association; she will be amply provided for out of the Church's funds. This is what I for my part recommend; but about taking the advice, you only are judge, for I am not compelling, but submitting the whole matter to your discretion."

The bishop's words do in fact compel the presbyter to admit what he has always known but has hitherto refused to acknowledge to himself, that his conduct is indefensible; faced with the facts he agrees that John's correction is justified and he promises to make arrangements for the young virgin to move immediately. Since their discussion has ended amicably, John turns to other matters, telling the presbyter that he has been going into the question of Church finance and is not satisfied with the contributions of the laity.

"During the course of your visiting you might suggest to the brethren that they make a small chest for the poor at home, putting it near the place where they are accustomed to pray; then as often as they go to pray, first let them deposit their alms and then offer up their petitions. I am also disturbed by the extent to which the Scriptures are being neglected."

"Yes, holy father, but when I urge them to read the sacred writings they reply, 'I'm not one of the monks, but I have both a wife and a child, and the care of a household.'"

"Why, that is what is ruining them all, their supposing that the reading of the Bible is a concern for the monks alone, when in fact they need it much more! For they that live in the world and each day receive wounds, these have more need of medicines. So that it is far worse than not reading, to account it even 'superfluous'; these are the words of the devil."

"They say that with work and family troubles they have no time to spare."

"Then tell them to read only a small portion; a little is better than none. Let them read the portion of the Gospel appointed for the Sunday so that they may at least be familiar with that."

"It is not an easy task, holy father."

"It certainly is not, and the prevalence of superstition makes it even harder to lead them forward in the way of holiness. How often one hears them saying, 'This or that man was the first to meet me as I walked out, consequently innumerable ills will certainly befall me; that confounded servant of mine, in giving me my shoes, handed me the left one first, this indicates dire calamities and insults; as I stepped out I started with the left foot foremost, this, too, is a sign of misfortune; my right eye twitched upwards as I went out, this portends tears. The braying of a donkey, the crowing of a cock, a sudden sneeze — all are omens of something. If one meets a virgin then one's journey will be barren, but if one meets a courtesan then it is certain to be fruitful.' "[28]

The conversation is interrupted by a great outcry from the street and, going to the door, John sees a crowd collected in front of the next house, while neighbors are hanging out of the windows.

"What is the matter there?" asks the bishop.

"Oh, she's beating her maid," answers a passer-by, and indeed from the shouting and weeping and wailing there can be little question of it. A cross on the door indicates that it is the home of one of the faithful, and without more ado John and his deacon make their way through the crowd and go in.[29]

"Thessalian witch! Runaway! Prostitute!" shrieks the irate mistress, beating the slave girl, whom she has stripped and tied to a pallet.

"What can be more shameless than this?" demands John sternly.

The mistress looks up in angry surprise, but though

[28] The prevalence of superstition was most marked; it led even to arduous pilgrimages, such as the journey by many to see Job's dunghill in Arabia (Chrysostom, *Ad Antioch.*, 5).

[29] The clergy were not allowed to visit women except in twos. (Ambrose, *De officiis ministrorum,* I, 87.)

she recognizes the bishop she is not prepared to stop her chastisement without an argument to justify herself.

"What, oughtn't one to give them a beating at all?"

"No, I'm not saying that, there may be occasions when it is permissible, but then it must be neither frequently nor to excess; nor should it be for any wrongs of your own, nor for any little failure in her service, but only if she has done harm to her own soul. If you chastise her for a fault of this kind, everyone will praise you, and there will be no one to upbraid you. But if you are doing it for any reason of your own, all will condemn your cruelty and harshness. Besides you are being so savage and lash her to such a degree that the bruises will last for many a day, and when she goes to the baths, and is naked, she will carry the marks of your cruelty. Ought these things to take place in a Christian household?"

"But they are a troublesome, audacious, impudent, incorrigible race."

"True, I am aware of that, but there are other ways to keep them in order; by threats, by words, which may touch her more powerfully and save you from disgrace. You who are a gentlewoman have uttered foul words, and you disgrace yourself no less than her."

"But the whole tribe of slaves is intolerable if it is met with indulgence."

"I agree, but then, as I was saying, correct them in

some other way, not by scourge only, but even by encouragement and by acts of kindness. If she is intemperate, cut off the temptations to drunkenness, call your husband and admonish her. Or do you not feel how disgraceful a thing it is for a woman to be beaten? They at least who have enacted ten thousand punishments for men — the stake and the rack — will scarcely ever hang a woman, but limit men's anger to slapping her on the cheek; and they have observed so great a delicacy towards your sex that not even when there is absolute necessity will they hang a woman, especially if she be pregnant. For it is a disgrace for a man to strike a woman; and if for a man, much more for one of her own sex."

"What then if she plays the harlot?"

"Marry her to a husband, cut off the temptations to fornication, do not let her be overindulged in food."

"And what if she steals?"

"Take care of her and watch her."

"What? Am I to be her keeper? How absurd!"

"And why aren't you to be her keeper? Hasn't she a soul as well as you? If she is a believer, she is your sister. Hasn't she been granted the same privileges by God? Doesn't she partake of the same table? Doesn't she share with you the same high birth?" [30]

"But what if she is a railer or a gossip or a drunkard?"

[30] The reference is to the Eucharist and to Baptism.

"How many free women aren't the same? God has charged men to bear with all the failings of women; only He says, let not a woman be an harlot, and bear every other failing besides. Yes, whether she be a drunkard, a railer, a gossip, evil-eyed, or extravagant or a squanderer of your substance, you have her as a partner for your life; you are bound to regulate her. You should do nothing so unworthy as this, nothing to disgrace yourself; set a bridle on your mouth. If you are disciplined to bear the provocations of a servant, you will not be annoyed with the insolence of an equal, and in being above annoyance you will have attained great heights of virtue. There is nothing more shocking than a woman in such a fit of rage; be an example, in everything be yourself a perfect pattern."

The bishop's prompt and vigorous protest has its effect and, having exacted a promise that she will try to control herself in future, he takes his leave and mounts his mule for the final journey back to his palace.

The streets are still crowded for the rich are now abroad; many of them have not left their embroidered beds until midday, stretching themselves out as if they were hogs in fattening, sitting on the edge of the bed, at first unable to move because of their previous night's debauch. And now dressed in silken robes they have been carried to sit in the hairdressers' and in the market place to gaze with many a yawn and bleary eyes at the passers-by. The ladies of fashion are to be seen, too, with their mincing gait, affected voices, languishing and wanton looks; their cloaks and bodices spangled with gold, their nicely wrought girdles and their sharp-pointed shoes polished with brilliant jet and ornamented with jewels. As they pick their way fastidiously on tiptoe to avoid staining their footwear with the mud, John feels like calling out in derision:

"Take and hang them from your necks, or put them on your heads!" [31]

Many of them are going in the same direction as the bishop, to the theater which is near the Kynegion, built by Severus for the exhibition of wild animals.

To John the theater is a seat of pestilence, the gymnasium of incontinence and a school ot luxury; Satan is the author and architect of it. Gross comedies, indecent ballets and ribald pantomime [32] are the rule; marriage is constantly mocked, even the Eucharist is burlesqued, and the *pièce de résistance* is the frolic of nude courtesans in a specially constructed swimming pool. Their songs are unashamedly coarse, with such themes

[31] Chrysostom made many scathing comments on the rich of his day. "When you are like an ass, kicking, and like a bull, wantoning, and like a horse neighing after women; when you play the glutton like the bear, and pamper your flesh as the mule, and bear malice like the camel; when you raven as a wolf, are wrathful as a serpent, sting like an asp or a viper, and war against your brethren like that evil demon; how shall I be able to number you with men, not seeing in you the marks of man's nature?" (*In Mtt. Hom.*, IV.)

[32] Few, if any, classical tragedies were now performed; cf. A. Puech, *St. Jean Chrysostome et les moeurs de son temps*, 1891, p. 269.

as that a woman loved a man and, not obtaining him, hanged herself. Indeed there is nothing in the conduct of the theatrical profession either on or off the stage which does not call forth the severest strictures of the Christian moralist.

It is a relief to quit the obnoxious scenes out of doors and return at last to his study, but as John takes up a codex and prepares to meditate a clamor breaks in upon him like the roaring of a storm at sea and he can hear the applause of the great men who are on the high tiers of seats mingled with the shouts of the mob below in the Hippodrome across the square. He can even distinguish individual cries.

"That horse didn't run fairly!"

"That horse was tripped and fell!"

The riotous and uncontrolled behavior that is taking place almost on his doorstep is familiar to the bishop: he knows the factions sporting the colors of the rival charioteers; he knows the heated debates of the horses' pedigrees and the calculation of their chances; he knows too the pathetic accidents which often take place, the severing of the head and extremities from the bodies of the unfortunate competitors caught between two chariots.

With an effort John recollects his thoughts and concentrates on the pages in front of him, refreshing himself for a short time with mental prayer, until he is disturbed by the entrance of the deaconess Olympias.

Knowing the bishop's tendency to forget his meals, often putting them off until the evening because of ecclesiastical matters or spiritual reading, she has made it her business to call each day with some barley bread. John is pleased to see her, for he is not a little worried about the widows and virgins and wishes to discuss their conduct with her.

"The present church, Olympias" (John introduces his subject) "is like a woman who has fallen from her former prosperous days, and in many respects only retains the symbols of that ancient prosperity; displaying indeed the caskets of her golden ornaments, but empty of wealth; that is what the present Church resembles. I am not referring to gifts, because there would be nothing marvelous in that if that were all that is amiss; but I refer also to life and virtue. Thus the lists of her widows and the company of her virgins then gave great ornament to the Church; but now she is made desolate and void and tokens only remain. There are indeed widows now, there are also virgins, but they do not retain that adornment which women should have who prepare themselves for such a life. For the special distinction of the virgin is both the caring for the things of God alone and the waiting on Him without distraction; and the widow's mark, too, should not be so much the not engaging in a second marriage as the other things — charity to the poor, hospitality, prayer. The married women exhibit among us great seemliness, but this is not the only thing required, but rather that careful attention to the needy through which those women of old shone out so brightly — not as the generality nowadays. For then, instead of gold, they were dressed with the fair garments of almsgiving; but now, having left off this, they are decked out on every side with cords of gold woven of the chain of their sins."

"It is only too true, holy father," agree Olympias. "Their very clothes reveal the shallowness of their spiritual life."

"Yes, the virgins study appearances in a common garment more than those who wear gold. For when a very dark-colored robe is drawn closely round the breast with the girdle, with such nicety that it may neither spread into breadth nor shrink into scantiness but be between both; and when the bosom is set off with many folds, this is just as alluring as any silken dresses. And when the shoe, shining through its blackness, ends in a sharp point, and imitates the elegance of painting so that even the breadth of the sole is scarcely visible — or when, though they do not indeed paint their faces, they spend much time and care on washing them and spread a veil across the forehead whiter than the face itself — and above that, put on a hood, of which the blackness may set off the white by contrast — isn't there in all this the vanity of dress? What can I say to the perpetual rolling of the eyes? To the putting on of the stomacher so artfully as sometimes to conceal, sometimes to disclose the fastening? For this, too, they sometimes expose to show the exquisiteness of the cincture, winding the hood entirely round the head. Then, like the players, they wear gloves so closely fitted that they seem to grow upon the hands. But this concern with the external is symptomatic of a far more serious lack of determination in their inner life; neither they nor the widows practice at home that discipline which is expected of them. It is the duty of virgins to live in the strictest privacy, not to parade the streets and to be in and out of other people's houses." [33]

"Unfortunately, holy father, many of them do not even avoid dinner parties."

"Indeed! Why the houses of the rich on those occasions are like the theaters, packed with parasites and actors with shaven heads and dancers jumping like camels, stuffing themselves with pork haggis and pheasants and gargling with Thasian wine. When they are at a loss for witty sayings, they indulge in the foul-

[33] St. Ambrose declares that "a virgin's adornment is absence of adornment" (*De virginibus,* i, 54) and, while accepting the white linen veil and dark-colored habit as the external signs of their profession, objected strongly to cosmetics for the face and curling irons for the hair (*De virginitate,* 71, 79). St. Jerome refers to the narrow purple stripe on the robe, to the headdress, somewhat loose so as to leave the hair free, to the lilac mantle, the *maforte,* fluttering from their shoulders, to their slippers and to their arms bound in tight-fitting sleeves (*Ep.,* XXII *ad Eustoch*). St. Augustine asserts: "There is a certain air of pleasing, either by more elegant dress than the necessity of so great a profession demands, or by remarkable manners of binding the hair, whether by bosses of hair swelling forth, or by coverings so yielding that the fine network below appears" (*De virgin.,* 34).

est oaths, and their conversation is of nothing but money, clothes and vice. Holy poverty has no place among all those vessels of gold and silver, those tablecloths of fine linen, those costly carpets and gilded draperies. The virgin should practice abstinence, not only in respect of meat and drink but also in respect of all worldly show, which is often more intoxicating than wine itself. She should start her day by reciting the Creed and continue in prayer, psalm-singing and the study of the Scriptures until she retires to bed, taking the Virgin Mary for her model, just as the widows should look up to holy Anna. And what I have been saying about the virgins equally applies to the widows; widowhood is not merely being free from a second marriage — it involves the renunciation of luxury and self-indulgence and the resolution to continue steadfast in prayers and supplications."

"There can be no question, holy father," comments Olympias, "that they are not living up to their high calling; many of them, I know, are guilty of the gravest misconduct."

"In that case I will summon the members of these orders [34] and investigate their conduct individually; if they wish to bring medical evidence they are entitled

[34] Virgins were duly consecrated to their order and adopted the veil, *flammeum Christi*, but the widows, who were not allowed to be enrolled under the age of sixty (*Ap. Const.*, III, 1), do not appear to have made any public profession in church. Cf. F. H. Dudden, *The Life and Times of St. Ambrose*, 1935, pp. 150–159.

to do so,[35] but no unpleasantness will prevent me from seeking to reform their behavior in accordance with the precepts of the Gospel.[36] You do not know, Olympias, the pangs of spiritual childbirth, how overpowering they are; how he who is in travail with this birth would rather be cut into ten thousand pieces than see one of those to whom he has given birth perishing and undone."

Before partaking of the frugal meal which Olympias has provided for him, John enjoys his daily bath in his private bathroom, for he has long since given up frequenting the public baths which provide open license for farmyard morality. The bishop eats alone, and soon finishes his rose water and bread, and says the concluding grace. Then he crosses for the second time this day to the church, where there is to be an evening service, arranged specially by John for the men who have been too busy during the day for any Christian devotions, and for an hour or more intercessions are offered and psalms are sung.

It is now quite dark when John re-enters his study and, taking a candle, he makes the sign of the cross be-

35 Where there seemed good reason to suspect a virgin of immorality, the bishop could order her to be medically examined, as in the case of Indicia (Ambrose, *Epp.*, 5, 6).

36 Chrysostom did indeed arraign them; he ordered some of the guilty to fast, some to abstain from public bathing, some from overdressing; otherwise they were to proceed without delay to marriage (Palladius, *Dial.*, V). On the punishment of virgins proved guilty of grave offenses, see *De lapsu virginis*, formerly attributed to Ambrose but now ascribed to Niceta of Remesiana.

fore lighting it and carrying it to his little table. He intends to resume his meditation interrupted before supper by Olympias, but interruptions are a normal feature of his day and he has no sooner settled down than the noise of a procession and of chanting brings him to the window. The words of the song are clear and distinct, and there is no question that this is a body of Arian heretics, Ario-maniacs, as the orthodox call them, singing one of their popular Thalias.[37]

God Himself then, in His own nature, is ineffable by all men;
Equal or like Himself He alone has none.
And Ingenerate we call Him, because of Him who is generate by nature;
We praise Him as Unoriginate because of Him who has an origin,[38]
And adore Him as everlasting, because of Him who in time has come to be.
The Unoriginate made the Son an origin of things generated;
And advanced Him as Son to Himself by adoption.
He has nothing proper to God in proper subsistence,
For He is not equal, no, nor one in substance with Him.
Wise is God, for He is teacher of Wisdom.[38]
Thus there is a Three, not in equal glories;
Not intermingling with each other are their subsistences.

[37] Convivial songs written in the style of Sotades and set to popular music.
[38] Christ.

One more glorious than the other in their glories unto
immensity.
Foreign from the Son in substance is the Father, for
He is Unoriginate.
Understand that the One was; but the Two was not,
before He was in existence.[39]
It follows at once that though the Son was not, the
Father was God.
Hence the Son, not being — for He existed at the will
of the Father —
Is God Only-begotten, and He is alien from either.
Wisdom existed as Wisdom by the will of the wise
God.
Hence He is conceived in numberless conceptions;[40]
Spirit, Power, Wisdom, God's Glory, Truth, Image
and Word.
To speak in brief, God is ineffable by His Son,
For He is to Himself what He is, that is unspeakable,
So that nothing which is called comprehensible
Does the Son know to speak about; for it is impossible
for Him
To investigate the Father, who is by Himself.
For the Son does not know His own substance,
For, being Son, he really existed at the will of the
Father.
What argument then allows, that He who is from the
Father
Should know His own parent by comprehension?
For it is plain that, for That which hath origin

39 Originally there was only One, God the Father; only when He created the Son were there Two in existence.

40 He is given titles corresponding to no reality.

To conceive how the Unoriginate is,
Or to grasp the idea, is not possible.

To John, the faithful bishop, the guardian of the purity of the Apostolic teaching, this is sheer blasphemy. To assert that Christ is a creature, that there was a time when He did not exist, is to deny the divinity of the Savior, to deny in fact the reality of redemption, to undermine the whole Christian Gospel and to remove all hope from the world.

Something must be done to counteract these demonstrations, there is no doubt about that; the only question is, what? Why not organize rival processions of the orthodox? He could design some silver crosses to bear lighted wax tapers; the empress will certainly give what assistance she can; he will seek an audience tomorrow and make the arrangements as quickly as possible.[41]

The chanting is growing fainter now as the Arians move off in the direction of the forum; they will probably continue until the early morning, but John, having made his decision, has no more thought for them and returns to his codex.

The voice of the night watchman as he passes along the now deserted streets tells John that it is time for bed, but before retiring he submits himself to a rigor-

[41] The Empress Eudoxia provided the crosses at her own expense, and her eunuch, Bruso, was detailed to superintend the procession. (Socrates, *Historia ecclesiastica,* VI, 8.)

ous self-examination, recalling his various activities throughout the day and making acts of penitence for his shortcomings. Then with the words of Psalm 141 on his lips:

> Lord, I have called upon thee; make haste unto me:
> Give ear unto my voice, when I call unto thee.
> Let my prayer be set forth as incense before thee;
> The lifting up of my hands as the evening sacrifice . . .

he lies down and is soon asleep.

> *There is nothing nowadays more easy, more agreeable, more desirable than the episcopate, the priesthood or the diaconate, if one's duties rest lightly and one occupies oneself in pleasing others; but before God there is nothing more miserable, more regrettable, more damnable. On the contrary nothing nowadays is more difficult, more arduous, more dangerous than the episcopate, the priesthood or the diaconate, but nothing is better in the eyes of God, if one fulfills the duties of this holy warfare according to the orders of the heavenly emperor.*[42]

[42] Aug., *Ep.*, XXI, *Ad Valerium.*

6

John Cassian, A Monk of Marseilles

A.D. 425

JOHN Cassian was born about the year A.D. 360, in Scythia, the district around the Danube Delta. Well educated by pious Christian parents, he forsook the world at an early age and together with his close friend Germanus entered a monastery at Bethlehem, which, as he tells us himself, "was at no great distance from the cave in which our Lord vouchsafed to be born of a Virgin." After several years, determined to make further progress in the monastic life, the two companions went to Egypt, the home of Anthony and Pachomius, the founders of the great movement, and there they passed the years from 386 to 399, visiting the different centers. For uncertain reasons, possibly because of the Origenist controversy, Cassian then went to Constantinople, where he was made deacon by St. John Chrysostom and, with Germanus, was placed in command of the treasury, the only part of the cathedral which escaped destruction in the great fire of 404. The following year, after Chrysostom's disgrace and exile, Cassian was the bearer of a letter to Rome from those who supported the patriarch, and there he was ordained priest. About 415 he settled at Marseilles, where he founded two monasteries — the one for men, built over the tomb of St. Victor, a martyr in the Diocletian persecution, the other for women. Here he wrote his three great works: the Institutes *in 425, which he describes as concerned with "what belongs to the outer man and the customs of the Caenobia," that is, the life and system of a monastery; the* Conferences, *426, whose subject was "the training of the inner man and the perfection of the heart," and finally, in 430,* On the Incarnation against Nestorius, *an attack upon an Eastern heresy which so divided the human and divine natures in Christ as to make of Him two persons. By his personal example and by the wide circulation of his first two works Cassian became the first organizer and systematizer of Western monasticism, but these same two works also involved him, in his turn, in the charge of heresy. In 433 St. Prosper of Aquitaine, an ardent supporter of St. Augustine, published a detailed criticism of the* Conferences *in which he maintained that Cassian was guilty of underestimating the necessity for divine grace to such an extent that he was almost a Pelagian — that is, a disciple of the British heresiarch who asserted that salvation lay within the power of each individual independent of any divine initiative or succor. Cassian made no reply and died two years later in 435, his reputation, which rested upon his services to the monastic movement and his profound spiritual insight revealed in his works, little impaired by this attack upon his orthodoxy.*

Standing in the courtyard of the St. Victor monastery, the monk on duty gazes up into the cloudless Mediterranean sky. He has been there for some time already, since he dare not depend on daily habit to awaken in time to summon his brethren to prayer. But as the stars tell him that it is now almost midnight, he moves quietly on sandaled feet along the porticoes tapping gently on the door of each cell in turn. John Cassian needs no second knock, and rising from his rush mat he immediately kneels and calls upon his Creator: "O God, make speed to save me: O Lord, make haste to help me." Divesting himself of the old shirt in which he has been sleeping, he puts on his short-sleeved linen tunic reaching to the knees, drawing it tight with a leather girdle; around his shoulders he drapes his *melote,* a length of sheepskin which hangs down at one side, and finally he slips his cowl over his head, a covering worn usually by children and adopted by the monks to symbolize the humility, purity and innocence they seek so ardently. The dress is unobtrusive, clean but commonplace, not calculated to attract attention.

The courtyard in which the monks are gathered for

Matins [1] is surrounded on three sides by covered porticoes; in the center of the fourth side there is a diminutive sanctuary, only a few square yards in area, built over the tomb of St. Victor. The service is divided into three parts to distribute the effort and to relieve bodily exhaustion, and it begins with three Psalms sung antiphonally, the brethren all standing. The Superior, John Cassian, upon whom devolves the discipline of the monastery, notices one or two monks entering after the chanting has begun, but since at this service late arrival is permitted up to the second Psalm, as long as the defaulter has taken his place before the Psalm is finished, he refrains from observation. Following the cantor, the monks prostrate themselves upon the ground after each "Gloria," and then stand upright, their arms outstretched, to pray.[2] It is the cantor, too, who plays the leading role in the second section of the service, for standing, he chants the first part of each verse of the next three Psalms, whilst the rest sit to sing the second half of each verse. Next, three lessons are recited from memory by those who are on duty for the week, and finally the congregation bows down once more in prayer. Unfortunately there are some who make haste to prostrate themselves before the last

[1] Cassian actually terms it "Nocturns," but the later, more familiar title is used here.

[2] The earliest recorded use of the "Gloria" is in the fourth century by St. Basil (*De Spiritu Sancto,* xxix); and the additional clause, "as it was in the beginning . . ." was not adopted in the West until the sixth century, being ordained by the Council of Vaison, 529.

words of Scripture have been uttered, in a hurry to finish the service as quickly as possible, while one old man, having once prostrated himself, remains there for a considerable time, not for the sake of prayer so much as for a rest. To these Cassian administers a gentle but timely rebuke and then returns to his cell, where he lies down to sleep once more.

At half past two Cassian is awake again and as he rolls up his rush mat he says: "O body, work that thou mayest be fed; O soul, rouse up that thou mayest inherit life." He is apt to make such ejaculations at all times of the day for since his aim, as he is wont humorously to express it, is to become "a sort of spiritual hedgehog," he seeks to occupy his mind wholly with God and to ward off all wandering thoughts. But although he must be barbed against all evil, vis-à-vis his fellow monks, Cassian strives to be gentle and conciliatory, for "he who sits among the brethren must not possess four corners, but he must be altogether round, so that he may move smoothly in respect of every man." Of course there are some who say that a monk's life is an idle one and that they have forsaken the world through laziness; to such Cassian quotes the answer he once heard from an old anchorite in Egypt: "Beloved, when the Ninevites, hearing the message of the prophet Jonah, were in need of repentance, which of them bothered about the demands of the world and its rights? So also it is with us, and because we have sinned against and transgressed the natural and written law we deny all the claims of the world until we shall see that reconciliation with God has taken place. Didn't St. Paul teach us this when he said: 'He who is fighting a battle keeps his mind free from everything else?'"

The ultimate end of the monk's endeavor is the kingdom of heaven, his immediate goal is purity of heart without which none can gain the ultimate end. It is this all-absorbing purpose which leads Cassian to fast and to practice every possible means of self-denial. Not that he is one who misses the wood for the trees, he knows that "fastings, vigils, meditations on the Scriptures, and the abnegation of all possessions are not perfection but aids to perfection." He abstains from certain things, not because they are evil in themselves but "because the passions are mighty and when they have waxed strong they kill us." It is humbleness of spirit which is above all necessary, for there are indeed "some monks who wear their bodies with the labors of abstinence and self-denial, and who, because they have not found understanding, are remote from the path of God." After all, "to drink wine with reason is better than to drink water with pride." On this road heavenward prayer is the principal helpmate and the soul's effort to be purged from sin is to enable it to pray, "for whatever our mind has been thinking of before the hour of prayer is sure to occur to us while we are praying, through the activity of the memory. Wherefore what we want to find ourselves like while we are praying, that we ought to prepare ourselves to be before the time of prayer. For the mind in prayer is formed by its previous condition, and when we are applying ourselves to prayer the images of the same actions and words and thoughts will dance before our eyes."

Cassian, an expert in the spiritual and devotional life, distinguishes four kinds of prayer, a distinction that he bases on the Apostle's dictum: "I exhort therefore first of all that supplication, prayers, intercessions, thanksgivings be made." By supplications, Cassian understands petitions concerning sin, in which one who is sorry for his present or past deeds asks for pardon. Prayers he interprets to mean vows, so that we pray when we renounce this world and promise that being dead to all worldly attractions we will serve the Lord with full purpose of heart, and we pray when we promise that despising secular honors and scorning earthly riches we will cleave to the Lord in all sorrow of heart and humility of spirit. Intercession is making request either for those dear to us or for the peace of the world, and, to use the Apostle's own phrase, we pray "for all men, for kings and all that are in authority." The final division of prayer is thanksgiving, the crown of all, which the mind in ineffable transports offers up to God, either when it recalls past benefits or when it contemplates God's present ones, or when it looks forward to those great ones in the future which God has prepared for those that love Him. Proficient in this last form, Cassian stands wrapped in contemplation, caught up by the Spirit Himself into the very life of the Holy Trinity, adoring without words, until the dull beating of a board summons him to the office of Lauds.[3]

The service follows the usual pattern, the special Psalms being numbers 148, 149 and 150, after each of which the cantor offers up prayers, and then Cassian retires once more to the peace and quiet of his cell, for "as a fish when it is lifted out of the water dies, even so does the monk who tarries outside his cell." Not that Cassian thinks that his mere physical presence within the four whitewashed walls is a guarantee of sanctity; on the contrary he knows only too well from experience that his body might obey the evangelic precept to enter into the chamber and shut the door, while his thoughts wander abroad in undisciplined fantasy with the danger of consequent depression and despair and the decision to return to the world as one who has no faculty for acquiring the rule of life which is proper to the monk. On such occasions Cassian reminds himself of the counsel he gives to so many novices who turn to him for help:

"You must know, my son, that this is a war of Satan, but go and continue in your cell, and do not leave it, and pray to God that He might give you the power to endure patiently, and then your mind will collect itself

[3] This was Cassian's Matins.

in you. For the matter is like that of a she-ass who has a sucking foal. If she be tied up, however much he may gambol about or wander hither and thither, he will come back to her eventually, either because he is hungry, or for other reasons which drive him to her; but if it happen that his mother be roaming about loose, both animals will go to destruction. And it is the same with regard to the monk; for if the body remain in the cell, the mind will certainly revert to it after all its wanderings, but if the body as well as the soul wander outside the cell, both will become a prey and a thing of joy to the enemy. For it is not an external enemy that we have to dread. Our foe is shut up within ourselves; an internal warfare is waged daily by us: and if we are victorious in this, all external things will be made weak, and everything will be made peaceful and subdued for the soldier of Christ."

Against such a foe, the weapon of meditation is ready to hand, its use deeply impressed upon him by his Egyptian teachers, and Cassian falls to his knees.

"How can I possess Thee, O Lord?" His lips move in noiseless supplication. "Thou knowest full well that I am a beast, and that I know nothing. Thou hast brought me to the prime of this life, deliver me for Thy mercy's sake; I am Thy servant and the son of Thine handmaiden, O Lord, by Thy will vivify Thou me."

He chooses for his subject the Lord's Prayer, pondering each clause, so wrapped in his exercise that he is immune to the calls of the world of which he has seen so much during his travels in the East.

> *Our Father* — When we confess with our minds that the God and Lord of the universe is our Father, we profess that we have been called from our condition as slaves to the adoption of sons; adding next *which art in heaven,* that by shunning with the utmost horror all lingering in this present life, which we pass upon this earth as a pilgrimage, we may the rather hasten with all eagerness to that country where we confess our Father dwells. To which state and condition of sonship when we have advanced, we shall be inflamed with the piety which belongs to good sons, so that we shall bend all our energies to the advance not of our own profits, but of our Father's glory, saying to Him: *Hallowed be thy name,* testifying that our desire and our joy is His glory. So when we utter these words we mean, "Make us, O Father, such that we may be able both to understand and take in what the hallowing of Thee is," or at least, "that Thou mayest be seen to be hallowed in our spiritual converse." And this is effectually fulfilled in our case when "men see our good works, and glorify our Father which is in heaven."
>
> *Thy kingdom come* — Either that whereby Christ reigns day by day in the saints (which comes to pass when the devil's rule is cast out of our hearts by the destruction of foul sins, and God begins to hold sway over us by the sweet odor of virtues) or else that which is promised in due time to all who are perfect, and to all the sons of God, when it will be said to them by Christ: "Come ye blessed of my Father, inherit the

kingdom prepared for you from the foundation of the world."

Thy will be done on earth as in heaven — What else is this but to ask that men may be like angels and that as God's will is ever fulfilled by them in heaven, so also all those who are on earth may do not their own but His will?

Give us this day our daily bread — That is the bread of heaven, the spiritual food which nourishes the soul and strengthens the heart of the inner man. It is the heavenly manna which we need, while it is still this day, while we are still pilgrims in need of sustenance in this present life.

Forgive us our trespasses as we also forgive them that trespass against us — O unspeakable mercy of God, which has not only given us a form of prayer and taught us a system of life acceptable to Him, but also gives us a power by which we can moderate the sentence of our Judge, drawing Him to forgive our offenses by the example of our forgiveness: when we say to Him: "Forgive us as we also forgive." And so without anxiety and in confidence from this prayer a man may ask pardon of his own offenses, if he has been forgiving toward his own debtors, and not towards those of his Lord. For some of us, which is very bad, are inclined to show ourselves calm and most merciful in regard to those things which are done to God's detriment, however great the crimes may be, but to be found most hard and inexorable exactors of debts to ourselves, even in the case of the most trifling wrongs. Whoever then does not from his heart forgive his brother who has offended him, by this prayer calls down upon himself not forgiveness but condemnation, and by his own profession asks that he himself may be judged more severely, saying: "Forgive me as also I have forgiven." And if he is repaid according to his own request, what else will follow but that he will be punished after his own example with implacable wrath and a sentence that cannot be remitted? And so if we want to be judged mercifully, we ought also to be merciful towards those who have sinned against us.

And lead us not into temptation — If we pray that we may not be suffered to be tempted, how then will our powers of endurance be proved, according to this text: "Everyone who is not tempted is not proved," and again, "Blessed is the man that endureth temptation"? The clause then, "Lead us not into temptation," does not mean this: Do not permit us ever to be tempted; but: Do not permit us when we fall into temptation to be overcome. *But deliver us from evil* — that is, do not suffer us to be tempted by the devil above that we are able, but "make with the temptation a way also of escape that we may be able to bear it."

The rays of the rising sun filter into the cell through the slitlike window, reminding Cassian that it is daybreak, and at the same time the summons to Prime [4] penetrates his concentration.

"Why do you hinder me, O Sun," he says in gentle

[4] Cassian's Second Matins. No account of the Eucharist is given, but it seems likely that there was a daily celebration in the monasteries of Gaul, unlike the East, where it took place in the monasteries only on Saturdays and Sundays; cf. Cassian, *Inst.*, VI, viii.

reproach, "who art arising for this very purpose, to withdraw me from the brightness of this true light?" [5]

On bare feet, for sandals are forbidden at the services, Cassian crosses the courtyard to his place. The silence is so complete that one would think there was no one present except the cantor, who stands to chant Psalm 51, but the short prayer that follows is interrupted by an absent-minded interjection from one monk inflamed with an uncontrollable and irrepressible fervor of spirit. The cantor, however, continues unconcerned with Psalms 62 and 90, and by the time the office has come to an end the courtyard is ablaze with the light of day.

This time the monks do not disperse, for a young man is to be admitted to the novitiate. He has already been lying outside the gate for ten days, as evidence of his perseverance and desire, as well as of humility and patience; and he is known to all the brethren who, on their way to work outside, have heaped scorn on him as he lay at their feet, to discover what he will be like in temptation by the way he has borne the disgrace. But since his ardor has remained unabated, he is brought in by the doorkeeper, who leads him before the Abbot, John Cassian.

"It is my duty as Superior of this monastery to put to you several questions. In the first place, are you a slave? For the Holy Church has decreed that no one may be

[5] The words are actually St. Anthony's (*Conf.*, IX, xxxi).

admitted who is a slave without his master's leave."

"I am not."

"Secondly, are you married? For, if so, you may not be admitted without the consent of your partner."

"I am not."

"Thirdly, have you committed any crime and for that reason are seeking refuge here?"

"No."

"Are you liable for any taxes still unpaid?"

"None whatsoever."

"Next, I must ask you whether you are in a position to forsake your relations and disregard any property which may belong to you?"

"I am."

"Have you any money still in your possession?"

"A few pence."

"Give them to the steward, who will return them to your relations, for we will not receive anything from you in case you should either feel pride at your gift or later demand its return. Now I must put you in mind of the rule of life which is observed here; later a more detailed explanation of it for your further understanding will be given, but you must know that entrance here involves poverty and unquestioning obedience to your superiors; we require silence at all times, unless express permission be given; attendance at all the services is obligatory; you must devote yourself continually to prayer and to fasting and have no contact with the outside world. Knowing something of what is required of you, are you prepared to accept this rule of life?"

"I am."

Cassian now gives orders for the young man to be stripped of his clothes and, as this is done, he explains the reason for it:

"From this you may learn not only that you have been despoiled of all your old things, but also that you have laid aside all worldly pride, and come down to the want and poverty of Christ, and that you are now not to be supported by wealth sought for by worldly means, but that you are to receive out of the holy and sacred funds of this monastery your rations for your service. As you know that you are to be clothed and fed in this way and that you have nothing of your own, you may learn not to be anxious about the morrow and may not be ashamed to be on a level with the poor, that is with the body of the brethren, with whom Christ was not ashamed to be numbered."

Cassian dresses the young man in the monastic habit and gives the clothes he has just discarded into the keeping of the steward.

"The steward will take care of these until you have proved yourself, and then they will be given to the poor; should you not persevere, however, they will be returned to you at your expulsion. Now if you will sit here at my feet, I will endeavor to say a few words to you which may be of help during the three years of your novitiate.

"You know that after lying so many days at the entrance you are today to be admitted. And to begin with you ought to know the reason for the difficulty put in your way. For it may be of great service to you in this road which you desire to enter if you understand the method of it and approach the service of Christ as you ought."

John clears his throat and then continues:

"You were for a long while refused by us, not as if we did not desire with all our hearts to secure your salvation, but for fear lest if we received you rashly we might make ourselves guilty of levity in the sight of God, and make you incur a yet heavier punishment if, when you had been too easily admitted by us, you had afterwards turned out a deserter or lukewarm. Therefore you ought in the first instance to learn the actual reason for renunciation of the world.

"Renunciation is nothing but the evidence of the cross and of mortification. And so you must know that today you are dead to this world, and that, as the Apostle says, you are crucified to this world and this world to you. Consider, therefore, the demands of the cross under the sign of which you ought henceforward to live in this life; because *you* no longer live, but *He* lives in you who was crucified for you. We must therefore pass our time in this life in that fashion and form in which

He was crucified for us on the cross so that we may have all our wishes and desires not subservient to our own lusts but fastened to His mortification. For so shall we fulfill the command of the Lord which says: 'He that taketh not up his cross and followeth Me is not worthy of Me.' But perhaps you will say: How can a man carry his cross continually? Or how can anyone who is alive be crucified? Hear briefly how this is."

A gentle breeze, blowing in from the Mediterranean, stirs the cypresses in the garden behind the chapel, but the monks do not look up; they are intent on the words of their Superior.

"The fear of the Lord is our cross. As then one who is crucified no longer has the power of moving or turning his limbs in any direction, so we also ought to affix our wishes and desires — not in accordance with what is pleasant and delightful to us now but in accordance with the law of the Lord, where it constrains us. For in this way we can have all our desires and carnal affections mortified."

Cassian's words flow on, uninterrupted by the brilliant red butterfly which alights on his shoulder for a brief instant.

"Take heed to continue even to the end in that state of nakedness of which you made profession in the sight of God and of His angels. In this humility, too, and patience, with which you persevered for ten days before the doors and entreated with many tears to be admitted into the monastery, you should not only continue but also increase and go forward. For it is too bad when you ought to go forward to perfection that you should begin to fall back to worse things. For not he who begins these things, but he who endures in them to the end shall be saved.

"The beginning of our salvation and the safeguard of it is the fear of the Lord. For through this those who are trained in the way of perfection can gain a start in conversion as well as purification from vices and security in virtue. And when this has gained an entrance into a man's heart it produces a contempt of all things, and begets a forgetfulness of kinsfolk and a horror of the world itself. But by contempt for the loss of all possessions humility is gained.

"That you may the more easily arrive at this, you must observe three things." Cassian numbers them on his fingers to give added emphasis to his words: "As the Psalmist says: 'I was like a deaf man and heard not and as one that is dumb who doth not open his mouth; and I became as a man that heareth not, and in whose mouth there are no reproofs,' so you also should walk as one that is deaf and blind. You should be like a blind man and not see any of those things which you find to be unedifying. If you hear anyone disobedient or disparaging another, you should not be led astray by such an example to imitate him, but 'like a deaf man,' as if you had never heard it, you should pass it all by. If insults are offered to you or wrongs done, be immovable, and as far as answer in retaliation is concerned be silent 'as one that is dumb.'"

The novice is beginning to show signs of a little restlessness in the growing heat of the morning; he has yet to acquire that detachment which characterizes the other brethren.

"But cultivate above everything else this fourth thing," Cassian's voice continues evenly, "which adorns and graces these three things of which I have just spoken; make yourself, as the Apostle directs, a fool in this world that you may become wise, exercising no judgment of your own on any of those matters which are commanded you, but always showing obedience, judging that alone to be holy which is God's law or the decision of your Superior declares to be such. For built upon such a system of instruction you may continue forever under this discipline, and not fall away from this monastery in consequence of any temptations or devices of the enemy." [6]

With these concluding words Cassian rises and dismisses the assembly, after committing the newcomer to the charge of the superintendent of the guesthouse. The novice will serve under this elder for a year and then, if his conduct has been satisfactory, he will be passed on to the dean and in company with nine other

[6] This address, abbreviated from *Inst.,* IV, xxxii–xlii, is worth reading in full because it expresses so clearly the purpose and ethos of the monastic calling.

juniors [7] will be further instructed in the monastic life. From the dean he will learn to conquer his own desires by performing those tasks which he finds most irksome, and so complete will be his obedience that he will only do those things which are expressly commanded, revealing his inmost thoughts and accepting his superior's judgment in all matters.

Crossing the courtyard, Cassian enters his cell, where he is shortly joined by the *hebdomadarii.* These are the weekly officers who entered on their duties on Monday morning after Matins, when the vessels and utensils were passed on to them; their turn will end on Sunday evening, after they have ceremonially washed the feet of all the brethren. They have come to receive their orders for the day from the Abbot, and Cassian instructs them to dust the sanctuary, to beat the mats and then to fetch clean clothes from the wardrobe and hand them out to those in need of them. After this, they are to collect some wood for the cooking, and then they are to go to the steward to be told what food to prepare for the meal. They have also to check the books in the library, collecting any which are no longer wanted.

One of them reports that he has found a buckle off a sandal and Cassian tells him to hang it up outside the sanctuary, leaving it there for three days; if it has not been claimed by the end of that time, then it is to be put in the wardrobe.

[7] Hence the derivation of the word "dean" from *decanus.*

"There is nothing further, brethren," says Cassian, "but before you go about your duties, let me tell you a little story to impress on you the need to do your work diligently. There was once a certain farmer who was exceedingly rich, and wishing to teach his sons farming he said to them, 'My sons, you see how I have become rich, and if you will be persuaded by me and will do as I have done, you will become rich also.' Then they said to him, 'Father, tell us how to become rich.' Now although the farmer knew that he who works always becomes rich, yet because he thought they might be lazy and not bother to work, he cunningly replied: 'There is one day in the year when if a man works he will become rich, but my memory is not what it was and I've forgotten the exact day; so you must work continually, and you mustn't be idle even for a day; in case that day is the lucky one and your work for the rest of the year be in vain.' So, brothers, if we labor and work each day, and do not give way to sloth, negligence and contempt, we shall find the way of life."

Left to himself, Cassian takes a codex of the Scriptures from the window sill. It is a matter for deep concern to him that the Bible is so little read.

"The prophets compiled the Scriptures," an Egyptian father once remarked to him, "and the Fathers have copied them, and the men who came after them learned to repeat them by heart; then this generation came and placed them in cupboards as useless things."

But the monks of St. Victor cannot be censured on this score; they spend many hours pondering the sacred writings. None of them indeed possess the prodigious memory of Ammonius of Nitria, who knows by heart both the Old and New Testaments, as well as the writings of Origen, Didymus, Pierius and Stephen, being able to recite six million lines, but all are well versed in Holy Writ. They do not bother with learned annotated editions, for as Cassian is wont to advise them, "If you seek to understand the Scriptures, do not read the commentators, but purify your hearts, for it is the veil of sin which leads to misunderstanding."

Cassian turns the pages slowly, weighing each word, moved from time to time to prayer, until at eight o'clock he dons his scapula, a large cape which serves as a working dress, puts on his sandals, and takes his staff from the corner.

The monks are collecting the week's washing from the wardrobe under the supervision of the dean, and when all are ready they troop out of the main gate. They walk a yard apart so that there is no temptation to talk, but an indistinct and incessant muttering accompanies them as each repeats under his breath a passage of Scripture or a Psalm he knows by heart. On arrival at the river, they kneel down along the edge and dip the clothes into the water; then, opening them, they pound them with stones to loosen the dirt, alternatively soaking and pounding until they are quite clean.[8] After spreading them out to dry in the sun, the monks return to the monastery; later they will fetch the clothes and carry them to their cells, where they will gently knead them with their hands until they are quite soft and supple.

Terce begins at nine o'clock, the third hour, reminding the brethren of the time when the Holy Spirit first descended on the Apostles assembled for prayer.

After the service the main manual work of the day takes place. Some of the older members of the community, who are past hard physical labor, spend the time in their cells, copying books, braiding ropes, or twisting fishing lines. Others, their leathern girdles replaced by cords, make their way to the garden behind the chapel, the foreman handing out the necessary tools as they go. There they will hoe the ground for vegetables, carrying dung to lay about the roots, clearing the water conduits, and attending to the fruit trees, the beehives and the cucumber beds. One of their number, whose duty it is to drive away the birds from the young crops, is notorious for his continual cry:

"Depart, O ye evil thoughts from within, and depart, O ye birds, from without!"

The amount of food which is grown in this way is

[8] This practice is still to be seen in the country districts of Provence, where the peasant women take their washing to the nearest stream.

considerably more than is needed for the monastery, but physical labor is deemed essential to achieve a balance between what is due to the outer man and what is profitable to the inner man, and out of the surplus the brethren provide for pilgrims and visitors, as well as putting aside a large store of provisions to give to those in prison or to distribute in times of famine.

In the workshops there is great activity — at the forge, at the carpenter's bench, at the shoe last, for many of the monks were skilled craftsmen [9] before they took their vows.[10] The articles they produce, apart from those used in the monastery, are sold to the local inhabitants, and a little group of monks is ready with some packages to go to the local fair. Accompanying them is a brother who is in charge of the wheat supply, for he has to negotiate with certain merchants. Since they will not return until after the meal, they are provided with some pickled vegetables and so, their muttered prayers hissing like their native cicada, they set out on their short journey, leaving a cloud of white dust behind them along the track.

[9] Palladius found in one monastery alone fifteen tailors, seven smiths, four carpenters, twelve camel drivers and fifteen fullers. (*Hist. Laus.*, xxxii.)

[10] Jerome (*Ep.*, XXII) refers to monks making a vow, and Basil (*Ep.*, CXC) asserts that the vow of celibacy was compulsory; what else was explicitly required at the beginning of the fifth century it is impossible to say, although poverty and obedience were probably already included. Cf. E. M. Pickman, *The Mind of Latin Christendom*, 1937, p. 473.

In the meantime the officers for the week are occupied about their household tasks. Some of them are in the bakery kneading the dough, which, after it has been in the oven, will be laid out in the sun to harden. Others are in the kitchen, lighting the fire before they clean and shred the vegetables to put in the pots to boil. Others again are trimming the lamps, sweeping the floors and laying the tables in the refectory; there are no idle hands and Cassian himself goes to the infirmary, where he tends the sick.[11] Later he retires to his cell and takes up his pen to continue his treatise on the monastic life which he is writing at the request of Castor, Bishop of Apta Julia, some forty miles due north of Marseilles, who wishes to introduce it into his diocese.

The dull thumping of the board calls the monks in from their work for Sext at midday, when uppermost in their thoughts is the crucifixion of their Lord which took place at this same sixth hour. The clear and harmonious voice of the cantor stirs up the minds of the brethren, increasing their fervor, so that the recitation of the Psalms becomes a vehicle of meditation. They absorb the thoughts of the Psalms and begin to sing them in such a way that they utter them with the deepest emotion of heart, not as if they are the compositions of the Psalmist, but rather as if they are their

[11] For a description of the kind of medical attention given, see pp. 176–178.

own utterances and their very own prayers. "They take them as aimed at themselves and recognize that the words were not only fulfilled formerly in the person of the prophet, but that they are fulfilled and carried out daily in their own case. For having experience of each state of mind in which each Psalm was sung and written, they become like their authors and anticipate the meaning rather than follow it; gathering the force of the words before they really know them, they remember what has happened to them, and what is happening in daily assaults when the thoughts of them come over them, and while they sing them they call to mind all that their carelessness has brought upon them, or their earnestness has secured, or Divine Providence has granted. All these feelings they find expressed in the Psalms so that by seeing whatever happens as in a very clear mirror they understand it better, and so instructed by their feelings as their teachers they lay hold of it as something not merely heard but actually seen. So their minds attain to incorruptible prayer which is not engaged on gazing on any image but is actually distinguished by the use of no words or utterances; but with the purpose of the mind all on fire is produced through ecstasy of heart some unaccountable keenness of spirit, and the mind being thus affected without the aid of the senses or any visible material pours it forth to God with groanings and sighs that cannot be uttered."

At the conclusion of the service, the monks enter the refectory, on the right-hand side of the court, and stand silently behind the benches in front of the long low tables, on which the *hebdomadarii* have already placed bread and salt. After the customary Psalm which serves as a grace, the brethren take their appointed places, their hoods drawn over their eyelids to prevent inquisitive glances and roving looks, so that they see nothing but the table immediately in front of them and their food. There is no prescribed amount for each individual to eat, since everyone should allow himself food according to the requirements of his strength or bodily frame or age, in such quantity as is required for the support of the flesh, and not for the satisfactory feeling of repletion. The food is such as is cheap and easily prepared, consisting of salted cherlock steeped in water, lentils, some leaves of boiled leeks, olives, and moistened beans. The menu varies little from day to day, although sometimes chopped garlic is served, and in the season boiled cabbage heads. They eat in silence, occasionally indicating by a movement of the hand to those on duty if they are in need of anything. Filling his little basin, Cassian helps himself to some oil from the cruse, making the sign of the cross over it as he does so, and munches reflectively, helping himself with his right hand only, as the lector begins to read.[12]

[12] This practice originated in Cappadocia, "not so much for the sake of the spiritual exercise as for the sake of putting a stop to unnecessary and idle conversation." (Cassian, *Inst.*, IV, xvii.)

The continuation of the Life of St. Martin by Sulpitius Severus. From that time quitting military service, Martin earnestly sought after the society of Hilary, bishop of the city of Poitiers, whose faith in the things of God was then regarded as of high renown, and in universal esteem. For some time Martin made his abode with him. Now this same Hilary, having instituted him in the office of the diaconate, endeavored still more closely to attach him to himself, and to bind him by leading him to take part in divine service. But when he constantly refused, crying out that he was unworthy, Hilary, as being a man of deep penetration, perceived that he could only be constrained in this way, if he should lay that sort of office upon him, in discharging which there should seem to be a kind of injury done to him. He therefore appointed him to be an exorcist. Martin did not refuse this appointment, from the fear that he might seem to have looked down upon it as somewhat humble. Not long after this, he was warned in a dream that he should visit his native land, and more particularly his parents, who were still involved in heathenism, with a regard for their religious interests. He set forth in accordance with the expressed wish of the holy Hilary, after being adjured by him with many prayers and tears, that he would in due time return. According to report, Martin entered on the journey in a melancholy frame of mind, after calling the brethren to witness that many sufferings lay before him. The result fully justified this prediction. For, first of all, having followed some devious paths among the Alps, he fell into the hands of robbers. And when one of them lifted up his axe and poised it above Martin's head, another of them met with his right hand the blow as it fell; nevertheless, having had his hands bound behind his back, he was handed over to one of them to be guarded and stripped. The robber, having led him to a private place apart from the rest, began to inquire of him who he was. Upon this, Martin replied that he was a Christian. The robber next asked him whether he was afraid. Then indeed Martin most courageously replied that he never before had felt so safe, because he knew that the mercy of the Lord would be especially present with him in the midst of trials. He added that he grieved rather for the man in whose hands he was, because, by living a life of robbery, he was showing himself unworthy of the mercy of Christ. And then entering on a discourse concerning Evangelical truth, he preached the word of God to the robber. Why should I delay stating the result? The robber believed; and, after expressing his respect for Martin, he restored him to the way, entreating him to pray the Lord for him. That same robber was afterwards seen leading a religious life; so that, in fact, the narrative I have given above is based upon an account furnished by himself.

During the course of this reading one of the brethren is heard weeping, but his companions take no notice, and all is quiet and orderly again by the time Cassian rises for the concluding hymn, which they all sing together:

Blessed be God, who nourisheth me from my youth up, who giveth food to all flesh: fill our hearts with joy and gladness, that we, having all sufficiency at all times, may abound unto every good work, through Jesus Christ our Lord, with whom be glory and honor and power to Thee, together with the Holy Spirit, forever and ever. Amen. Glory to Thee, O Lord! Glory to Thee, Holy One! Glory to Thee, King, who hast given us food to make us glad! Fill us with the Holy Spirit, that we may be found well pleasing in thy sight, and not ashamed when Thou rewardest every man according to his works.

As the monks file out of the refectory Cassian signals to two of them to stay behind.

"Why, brother," he asks the first, "did you disturb our peace with tears?"

"Because, father, I shrink from partaking of irrational food, being myself rational destined to live in a paradise of delight owing to the power given us by Christ."

"Remember, a reasonable supply of food partaken of daily with moderation is better than a severe and long fast at intervals."

With this cryptic dismissal, Cassian turns to the second monk, of whose gluttony he has been an unavoidable witness since he was sitting opposite him.

"Brother, let me set you a puzzle. My father left me in the clutches of a great many creditors. All the others I have paid in full, and have freed myself from all their pressing claims; but one I cannot satisfy even by a daily payment."

"I do not perceive the meaning, father."

"I was," replied Cassian, "in my natural condition, encompassed by a great many faults. But when God inspired me with the longing to be free, I renounced the world, and at the same time gave up all my property which I had inherited from my father, and so I satisfied them all like pressing creditors, and freed myself entirely from them. But I was never able altogether to get rid of the incentives to gluttony. For though I reduce the quantity of food which I take to the smallest possible amount, yet I cannot avoid the force of its daily solicitations, but must be perpetually dunned by it, and be making as it were interminable payments by continually satisfying it, and paying never-ending toll at its demands. Yet we must continually fight against this sin, for if a king wishes to subdue a city belonging to enemies, he first of all keeps them without bread and water, and the enemy being thus harassed by hunger becomes subject unto him; and so it is in respect of the hostile passions, for if a man endures fasting and hunger regularly, his enemies become stricken with weakness in the soul. Now go in peace, brother, and say this prayer from your heart: 'I, O Lord, like a man, have sinned, and do Thou, like God, forgive me.' "

Recrossing the courtyard Cassian meets one of the novices who is usually most assiduous in seeking his spiritual counsel, but who recently has not made his appearance so regularly, so he stops and questions him about it.

"I fear to come too often, father, in case it wearies you."

"I see," says Cassian gravely. "Now go and bring a lamp to my cell."

In a few minutes the young man is back and is told to light the lamp and then to fetch several others.

"I have done as you order, father."

"Good; light the others from the first one. . . . Now is the lamp from which you have kindled the others in any way the worse?"

"No."

"If all the brethren were to come to me for spiritual comfort, I should be none the worse for it, neither would the gift of the grace of God be impeded thereby. So whenever you wish and are in doubt come to me."

As the novice leaves the cell the dean enters, revealing by his manner some concern, for Cassian has summoned him to answer a complaint that he is too harsh towards the younger men who, by the rule of the monastery, are compelled to disclose all their thoughts to him.

"Brother." Cassian's tone is stern. "I will tell you a story to emphasize the need for sympathy and charity in your relationship with the young. There was once a young man who went to an elder for the sake of the profit and health of his soul, and he candidly confessed that he was troubled by carnal appetites and the spirit of fornication, fancying that he would receive from the old man's words consolation for his efforts and a cure for his wounds. The old man attacked him with the bitterest reproaches and called him a miserable and disgraceful creature, and unworthy of the name of monk while he could be affected by a sin and lust of this character. Instead of helping him, he so injured him by his reproaches that he dismissed him from his cell in a state of hopeless despair and deadly despondency.

"And when he was plunged in deep thought, no longer how to cure his passions, but how to gratify his lust, the Abbot met him, and seeing by his looks and gloominess his trouble, asked him the reason for this upset; and when he could not possibly answer the Superior's gentle inquiry, the old man began to ask still more earnestly the reasons for his hidden grief. And by this he was forced to confess that he was on his way to a village to take a wife, as the old man had told him he could not be a monk if he was unable to control the desires of the flesh and to cure his passion. Then the Abbot smoothed him down with gentle words and told him that he himself was daily tried by the same pricks of desire and lust, and therefore he ought not to give way to despair and he begged him to put off his intention and return to his cell. The young man complied, comforted, and the Abbot then stretched forth his hands and prayed with tears: 'O Lord, who art alone the righteous judge and unseen physician of secret strength and human weakness, turn the assault from the young man upon the old one, that he may learn to condescend to the weakness of sufferers, and to sympathize even in old age with the weaknesses of youth.' Immediately the old man came out of his cell and ran about hither and thither like a lunatic or a drunkard and then, no longer able to restrain himself, set off in haste in the same direction the young man had taken. Then the Abbot came up to him and said: 'Where are you hurrying, and what has made you forget the gravity of your years and disturbed you in this childish way, and made you hurry about so rapidly?' He did not venture a reply, realizing that the Abbot was aware of his lust, so the Abbot said: 'Return to your cell and accept the fact that the Lord has allowed you to be tempted that you may at least learn in your old age to sympathize with infirmities to which you are a stranger, and may know from your own experience how to condescend to the frailties of the young, never terrifying with destructive despair those who are in danger, nor hardening with severe speeches, but rather restore them with gentle and kindly consolation!' Remember the grief of one in trouble ought never to be lightly despised."

The dean is followed by another monk who is disturbed by the instability of his devotions.

"Why is it, father, that as I sit in my cell I am sometimes filled with the utmost gladness of heart, together with inexpressible delight and the holiest of feelings, so that I will not say speech but even feeling cannot follow it, and pure prayers are readily breathed, and my mind being filled with spiritual fruits, praying to God even in sleep, can feel that its petitions rise lightly and powerfully to God: and again why is it that for no reason I am suddenly filled with the utmost grief, and weighed down with unreasonable depression, so that I not only feel as if I myself am overcome with such feelings, but also my cell grows dreadful, reading palls upon me, and my very prayers are offered up unsteadily and vaguely; so that while I am groaning and endeavoring to restore myself to my former disposition, my mind is unable to do it, and the more earnestly it seeks to fix again its gaze on God, so it is the more carried away to wandering thoughts?"

"A threefold account," answers Cassian, "of this mental dryness of which you speak has been given by the elders. For it comes either from carelessness on our part, or from the assaults of the devil, or from the permission and allowance of the Lord. From carelessness on our part when, through our own faults, coldness has come upon us, and we have behaved hastily, and owing to slothful idleness have fed on bad thoughts and so made the ground of our heart bring forth thorns and thistles, which spring up in it and consequently make us sterile, and powerless as regards all spiritual fruit and meditation. From the assaults of the devil when sometimes while we are actually intent upon good desires, our enemy with crafty subtlety makes his way into our heart, and without our knowledge and against our will we are drawn away from the best intentions. From the permission and allowance of the Lord when He chooses to prove our perseverance and steadfastness of mind and showing us the weakness of our hearts to teach us humility."

"But my thoughts continually vex me."

"Then," comments Cassian tersely, "spread out your robe and catch the wind."

"I cannot do that."

"Agreed, you cannot do that; neither can you prevent evil thoughts from coming, but it is for you to withstand them."

So the early afternoon passes away as Cassian fulfills his role of spiritual director, now with a word of rebuke, now with gentle encouragement, his remarks spiced with a certain dry humor, as he analyzes the spiritual condition of his consultants, lays bare the origin of individual sins and suggests possible remedies.

At three o'clock, the ninth hour, when Our Lord yielded up His spirit, the community assembles for the service of None. In low reverent tones the brethren join in the responses, but the clear voice of the cantor is abruptly silenced by the clapping of Cassian's hands, for the Psalms are divided into sections of ten verses and the young monk has absent-mindedly exceeded the appointed number. At the Abbot's sign all rise for prayer and the office continues smoothly to its end.

At this moment the steward approaches Cassian with the news that some visitors have arrived, in company with the brethren who have returned from the market. This is an occasion for the relaxation of the normal strict routine of the monastery and the guests are welcomed hospitably; towels and basins are brought and their feet are washed.[13] The newcomers include monks from the island of Lerins [14] and several sailors who have recently returned from a voyage to Asia Minor; the former express some surprise at the eagerness with which they have been greeted, supposing that their visit would rather be considered tiresome.

"Oh no," answers Cassian, "unless the strain of our minds is eased by the relaxation of some changes, we may fall either into a coldness of spirit, or at least into a most dangerous state of bodily health. Let me illustrate my point with an old story about the Evangelist John. It is said that the blessed John, while he was gently stroking a partridge with his hands, saw a hunter who was astonished that a man of so great fame and

[13] The monks themselves had no baths. (Jerome, *Ep.*, CXXV.)

[14] Cassian sent copies of his *Conferences* to the island, as well as dedicating a section to Honoratus, the founder.

reputation should demean himself to such paltry and trivial amusements, and said: 'Can you be that John whose great reputation attracted me with the desire to make your acquaintance? Why then do you occupy yourself with such poor amusements?' The blessed John replied: 'What is that you are carrying in your hand?' 'A bow.' 'And why do you not carry it everywhere bent?' 'Because,' the hunter replied, 'it would not do, the force of its stiffness would be relaxed by its being continually bent, and when it was time to shoot arrows after some beast its stiffness would be lost by the excessive and continuous strain.' 'And, my lad,' said the blessed John, 'do not let this slight and short relaxation of my mind disturb you, as unless it is sometimes relieved and relaxed by some recreation, the spirit would lose its spring owing to the unbroken strain, and would be unable when need required implicitly to follow what is right."

"You have answered our inquiry so courteously, father, that I am tempted to ask you something further," one of the monks says. "At Lerins we are accustomed to spend the whole of our day in prayer, seldom leaving the huts and caves in which we live; but I see that some of the brethren here are on their way to the garden to work. Surely such activity is detrimental to the true monastic life?"

"I remember once hearing a story about the Abbot Silvanus who lived near Mount Sinai, a story which is most apposite to your question," answers Cassian. "A stranger monk came to the Abbot and saw the brethren busy in the fields and said to them, 'Wherefore do you labor for the meat that perisheth? For Mary chose that good part.' Then said the old man to Zachary his disciple: 'Give him a codex to read and put him in a cell that has nothing in it.' By the ninth hour, however, the brother was gazing up and down the road, to see if perchance the old man would call him to a meal. And when the hour had gone by, he came to the old man and said, 'Are the brethren not eating today, father?' And when the old man said they were: 'Why,' said he, 'did you not call me?' Then said the Abbot Silvanus, 'You are a spiritual man, and you do not hold food to be necessary; but we being carnal have need to eat, and to that end we work; but you have chosen that good part. For you read all day and have no wish for carnal food.' And on hearing this he began to be ashamed and said, 'Forgive me, father.' And the Abbot Silvanus answered him, 'So Martha is necessary to Mary, for because of Martha is Mary praised.' "[15]

The conversation continues pleasantly for some little time until Cassian intimates that he must go about his duties. But first he escorts them to the guesthouse, to the left of the gateway, telling them that they are at liberty to remain as long as they like; if, however, they should stay longer than a week, then they will be ex-

[15] St. Augustine's treatise *De opere monachorum* is concerned with this same problem of monks who expect to do no work but to be entirely supported by the offerings of the faithful.

pected to help in the garden, the bakery or the kitchen.

The Abbot next interviews those of his monks who have just come back from market, inquiring what they have done, whom they have seen and what conversation they have held.

"Father," reports one of them, more anxious for praise than anything else, "I met certain of the handmaids of God from our sister monastery, so I turned aside out of the way."

"If you had been a perfect monk you would not have looked so close as to perceive that they were women."

After Cassian's cross-examination, the brethren hand over to the steward their various purchases together with the money which they have received from the sale of their goods.

The steward reckons it up, counting all the tens to ninety on his left hand and then at a hundred crossing over to his right; at the conclusion of his addition he addresses Cassian:

"Father, this brother will never prosper by such acts as these, for he still has a worldy mind."

"In what way has he behaved badly?"

"I gave him sandals and some other leather goods to sell and I told him that their price was so much, but he has sold them for a great deal more and has brought me a price which is three times as large as that which I mentioned to him."

"Why did you do this, brother?"

"Father, I told the people who bought the goods the price which the steward told me to take, and they said that they had been stolen, otherwise they would be worth a higher price than I was asking; and I, feeling ashamed, said that they had not been stolen, but that they could give me what they liked, and here it is."

"You have been guilty of a grave sin, but run quickly and give back the excess in price to those who gave it you, and come and repent because of this excess. In future you will remain in the monastery. It is not good, my son, that you should do this kind of task again."

Just before Cassian dismisses them he is given a large packet of letters which they have collected from the town, and in some distress of mind he goes to his cell. It is over fifteen years since he has heard of his father and mother, and now here is a whole sheaf of news from them.

"What thoughts," he muses to himself, "will the reading of these suggest to me, which will incite me either to senseless joy or to useless sadness! For how many days will my attention be distracted from the contemplation I have set before me by the recollection of those who wrote them! How long will it take for the disturbance of mind thus created to be calmed, and what an effort it will cost for that former state of peacefulness to be restored, if the mind is once moved by the sympathy of the letters, and by recalling the looks of those whom it has left for so long begins once more in thought and spirit to revisit them, to dwell among them and to be with them. And it will be of no use to have forsaken them in the body, if one begins to look on them with the heart, and readmits and revives the memory which on renouncing this world everyone gave up, as if he were dead."

Turning this over in his mind, Cassian determines not only not to read a single letter, but not even to open the packet, for fear lest at the sight of the names of the writers his purpose might be weakened. So without more ado, he goes to the kitchen and throws the bundle into the fire,[16] all tied up just as he has received it, crying: "Away, you thoughts of my home, be burned up, and try no further to recall me to those things from which I have fled."

Passing along one of the porticoes, Cassian goes to visit a certain brother;[17] reaching the door he pauses, and to his surprise hears him muttering animatedly. He stands still for a moment, wanting to know what it is that he is reading from the Bible or repeating by heart, but he finds that the monk is actually delivering a sermon to an imaginary congregation. When the dis-

16 This anecdote typifies the customary attitude of the monk (cf. Basil, *Regulae fusius tractatae,* XXXII), but by way of contrast there is the story of the one who, after fifty years in a monastery, heard that his mother was constantly annoyed by creditors and trebled his manual labor, so relieving her of the burden of debt. (*Inst.,* V, xxxviii.)

17 No monk may visit another before the ninth hour. (Jerome, *Ep.,* XXII.)

course is finished Cassian enters and is asked in some confusion how long he has been outside the door.

"I only arrived while you were giving out the dismissal of the catechumens," is the cryptic reply.[18] "But you should be ashamed of yourself to indulge in such a spirit of vainglory. Let me remind you of something that should be familiar to you, the advice which the Abbot Macarius once gave to a brother who was similarly afflicted. The young man came to his superior and said, 'Father, speak to me a word whereby I may live.' Abbot Macarius said to him, 'Go to the cemetery and blaspheme the dead'; and he went and blasphemed them and threw stones at them, and came and informed the old man. 'Did they give you answer?' 'No.' And the Abbot said, 'Go tomorrow and praise them'; and he came and said, 'I have praised them.' 'Did they say nothing to you?' 'Nothing.' And the Abbot said, 'You see how you have praised them and they returned no answer, and that although you reviled them they said nothing. And so let it be with you. If you wish to live, become dead, so that you may care neither for the reviling of men nor for their praise, for the dead care for nothing; in this way you will be able to live.'" Cassian pauses. "The subtle attacks of pride are not familiar to nor experienced by most men, because the majority

[18] In modern usage one would say: "As you were giving the blessing," or "As you were giving out the offertory sentence." See the account of the Eucharist in the previous chapter for the distinction between the Mass of the catechumens and the Mass of the faithful.

do not aim at attaining perfect purity of heart, so as to arrive at the stage of these conflicts. With you, however, this is not so, and as a remedy against these temptations I recommend you to bear constantly in mind the passion of Our Lord and all His Saints, considering that the injuries by which we are tried are so much less than theirs, as we are so far behind their merits and their lives; remembering also that we shall shortly depart out of this world, and soon by a speedy end to our life here become sharers of their lot. I had come to ask you if you would lead our Spiritual Conference tonight, but instead I must order you to do penance at Vespers in the usual manner."

At Vespers, the offending monk lies prostrate with his forehead touching the ground, performing his public penance, not permittd to join in the prayers nor receiving absolution until at the end of the service by the Abbot's command he is bidden to rise.

Cassian's ensuing meditation arises from the passage of St. Martin's life which he has heard at the midday meal. Reflecting first upon the saint and his spiritual victories, Cassian attains to consideration of God alone, going beyond the actions and services of the saint and feeding on the beauty and knowledge of God Himself.

The monks are accustomed to only one meal a day, but at seven o'clock Cassian repairs to the refectory for supper, specially provided for the guests. The visitors from Lerins are somewhat surprised to see the Abbot eating with them and they ask why it is that he has broken the daily fast without scruple.[19]

"The opportunity for fasting," Cassian explains, "is always with me; but I cannot always keep you with me. And a fast, although it is useful and advisable, is yet a freewill offering. But the exigencies of a command require the fulfillment of a work of Charity. And so receiving Christ in you, I ought to refresh Him; but when you have gone on your way, I shall be able to balance the hospitality offered for His sake by a stricter fast on my own account. For 'the children of the bride-chamber cannot fast while the bridegroom is with them': but when he has departed, then they will rightly fast."

Not that the Abbot and his guests, even on this occasion, are sitting down to a sumptuous feast; their menu consists of a porridge of lentils, three olives each, five grains each of parched vetches, two prunes and a fig, bread and a little oil for the vegetables. As they eat the plain fare, Cassian advises them that immediately after supper there will be a Spiritual Conference and he is asked by one of the sailors to explain its purpose.

"You would agree that it is dangerous to jump to conclusions and lay down the law hastily about any-

19 The custom was one meal a day, which on station or fast days (Wednesdays and Fridays) was at the ninth hour, on other days at the sixth. Supper also was allowed on Saturdays, Sundays and holy days. (*Inst.*, III, xii.)

thing before you have properly discussed the subject. Nor should you, looking only at your own weaknesses, hazard a conjecture, but should be in a position to pronounce a judgment based on the practice itself and on others' experience of it. Let me explain the point by means of an illustration with which you, as a sailor, will be familiar. If anyone who was ignorant of swimming, but knew that the weight of his body could not be supported by water, supposed that no solid body at all could be supported on it, we ought not to think his opinion correct; for though it is in accordance with his own limited experience, it can be shown by others to be entirely false. So in a Spiritual Conference we share our experience of the spiritual life. Besides, the human mind is very unstable and quite incapable of remaining idle, and unless provision is made for it, it must by its own fickleness wander about and stray over all kinds of things; in a Spiritual Conference provision is made for it, the mind being presented with material which will not distract it but serve to discipline it and concentrate it more on God."

In the courtyard the monks are already sitting on their mats when Cassian and the visitors take their places. At a sign from the abbot, one of the elders rises and begins his address: [20]

[20] It would have been more appropriate to have given one of the Conferences reported by Cassian himself, but they are too long for inclusion here and a paraphrase would do them less than justice, so a shorter address recorded by Anan-Isho is printed instead. (*The*

Our visitors, as I understand, are anxious to know something of the life of a monk, and so my words will be directed to giving an account of this blessed way. I counsel you to take the yoke of pleasantness upon your neck, for it will help you to sit by yourself in silence, and to withdraw yourself from human intercourse, and from cares about the things of this world which will hinder you. Make yourself as the dust in your humility towards every man, knowing at the same time that there is hope for you. And let not weeping cease from your eyes, for there is the occasion of tears. Make your cell a hall of judgment of yourself, and a place for striving against devils and evil passions, and let there be depicted therein the kingdom of heaven, and hell, and death and life, and sinners and the righteous, and the outer darkness, and the gnashing of teeth, and the joy of the righteous in the Holy Spirit, and the Passion of our Lord, and the memorial of His Resurrection, and the redemption of creation. Let your habitation be free from superfluous things, for one of two things will happen to you: either through thinking of them you will suffer injury, or in withdrawing yourself from them your war will be added to and become fiercer. Take heed lest through holding in honor and sparing other folk, you bring yourself to evil case in the war; whatever belongs to lust and is of the eyes you shall not possess, for the wars of your passions are sufficient for you. Heal yourself and make whole in your habitation those in whom God has pleasure; it is He that knows your sitting down and your coming in, and

Book of Paradise, trans. Budge, 1904, "Questions and Answers on the Ascetic Life," 579.)

your going out. In all your conduct be constant in prayer, especially in the night seasons, for night is the acceptable time for prayers, as it is written: "Be thou like unto thy Lord, who prayed to God continually throughout the night until the rising up of the sun." When all voices are quiet fill your mouth with praise, and your tongue with glorifying, and while others are lying like dead men on their biers do you depict in yourself the waking of the Resurrection. The night which is darkness to other folk shall be to you as bright as the day, and instead of filling yourself with wine as other men do, fill yourself with the love of God; and in the night season, when silver and gold are stolen, do you steal the kingdom of heaven like a thief. In the night season when sinners perform their evil deeds to their own injury, do you labor for the benefit of your own soul, and take care continually of all excellencies. Then He who is merciful in His gifts, and rich unto everyone who calls upon Him, will come unto you quickly and will help you, and you shall smite the Evil One, and shall bring his crafty acts to nothing. You shall make your mind to shine, and the Lord of all shall place in you the innocent thoughts of uprightness, and He shall comfort your mind. Then shall the rugged ground become smooth before you, and the difficult ground shall be as a plain, and your ship shall anchor in its haven. And you shall lead beforehand the life which is to come, and you shall fulfill the will of God, according to His will, both in heaven and on earth; and your knowledge shall grow and your joy increase in proportion to your spiritual conduct; and you shall be held to be worthy of the sight of the righteous by the grace and mercy of Christ our Lord, to whom, with His Father and the Holy Spirit, be glory now, and always and forever and ever. Amen.

The evening is beginning to close in as Cassian returns finally to his cell. His devotions are not yet concluded, however, and he kneels to examine his conscience, going over the actions of the day, trying to recall if he has been guilty of evil thoughts, if he has been inattentive during the Psalms, if he has allowed any desire for the world to flit across his mind, offering up his shortcomings one by one to God, praying that his wrongs may be healed and his sins forgiven, his tears of contrition mutely pleading with his Heavenly Father for pardon.

At last, wearily, he unrolls his mat, takes off his habit and lies down to sleep,[21] his lips moving in petition so to grow in spiritual stature that he may be numbered with "those choirs of saints who shine like brilliant stars in the night of this world" — his brethren, the monks.

Of what consisteth the life of a monk? A mouth of truth, a holy body, and a pure heart.[22]

[21] The monks only allowed themselves four hours' sleep a day (*Conf.*, XIII, vi) so Cassian has two hours till midnight and the remaining two after Nocturns.

[22] Anan-Isho, *The Book of Paradise,* trans. Budge, 1904, "Sayings," II, 465.

APPENDIX I

Authorities

1. *Clement, A Philosopher of Alexandria*

Clark, J. W., *The Care of Books,* 1901
Clement, *Opera*
Cyprian, *De opere et eleemosynis*
Eusebius, *Historia ecclesiastica*
Forster, E. M., *Alexandria: A History and a Guide,* 1938
Gregory Thaumaturgus, *In originem oratio panegyrica*
Hippolytus, *Apostolic Tradition*
Justin, *Apologia*
Lassus, J., *Sanctuaires chrétiens de Syrie,* 1947
Lucian, *Vota seu navigium*
Mommsen, T., *The Provinces of the Roman Empire,* 1886
Neroutsos-Bey, *L'ancienne Alexandrie,* 1888
Ovid, *Tristia*
Origen, *De oratione*
Pliny, *Historia naturalis*
Philo, *De legatione ad Gaium*
Rogers, C. F., *Baptism and Christian Archaeology (Studia Biblica et ecclesiastica,* V, pt. iv), 1903
Rostovtzeff, M., *Dura-Europos and Its Art,* 1938
Seyffert, O., *A Dictionary of Classical Antiquities,* edited by H. Nettleship and J. E. Sandys, 1895
Tertullian, *Opera*
Tollinton, R. B., *Clement of Alexandria,* 1914

2. *Paul, A Heretic of Antioch*

Antioch-on-the-Orontes, Reports of Princeton University Expedition, 1934 onwards
Bouchier, E. S., *A Short History of Antioch,* 1921
Clement, *Opera*
Eusebius, *Historia ecclesiastica*
Frank, Tenney, ed., *An Economic Survey of Ancient Rome,* 1938, vol. iv
Gibbon, Edward, *The History of the Decline and Fall of the Roman Empire,* 1776–1788
Hefele, C. J., *A History of the Christian Councils,* I, 1894
Kidd, B. J., *A History of the Church to* A.D. *461,* i, 1922
Lawlor, H. J., "The Sayings of Paul of Samosata," *J. T. S.,* XIX, 1918, pp. 20–45, 115–120
Loofs, F., *Paulus von Samosata,* 1924
Marquardt, J., *La vie privée des Romains,* I, 1892
Mommsen, T., *The Provinces of the Roman Empire,* 1886
Pliny, *Historia naturalis*
Réville, A., *"Le Christianisme unitaire au troisième siècle — Paul de Samosate et Zénobie,"* *Revue des Deux Mondes,* LXXV, 1868, pp. 73–106
Sozomen, *Historia ecclesiastica*
Tertullian, *Opera*
Tucker, T. G., *Life in the Roman World,* 1910

3. *Victoria, A Martyr of Carthage*

Allard, P., *Histoire des Persécutions,* 1886
Apostolic Constitutions
Asterius, *Oratio,* xi
Audollent, A., *Carthage romaine,* 1901
Cagnat, R., *Carthage, Timgad, Tebessa et les Villes Antiques de L'Afrique du Nord,* 1907
Cyprian, *De exhortatione martyris*

Dix, G., *The Shape of the Liturgy,* 1945
Eusebius, *Historia ecclesiastica* and *De martyribus Palestinae*
Gebhardt, O. v., *Acta martyrum selecta,* 1902
Jennison, G., *Animals for Show and Pleasure in Ancient Rome,* 1937
Knopf, R., and G. Krueger, *Ausgewählte Märtyrakten,* 3rd ed., 1929
Lactantius, *De mortibus persecutorum*
Mason, A. J., *The Historic Martyrs of the Primitive Church,* 1905
Origen, *In Jeremiam, Homiliae* xiv, and *Ad martyras*
Owen, E. C. E., *Some Authentic Acts of the Early Martyrs,* 1927
Papeyre, G. G., and A. Pellegrin, *Carthage, Latine et Chrétienne,* 1950
Prudentius, *Peristephanon*
Ruinart, *Acta primorum martyrum sincera,* 2nd ed., 1713
Tertullian, *Apologeticus; Ad nationes; Ad martyras;* and *De spectaculis*
Workman, H. B., *Persecution in the Early Church,* 1906

4. *Diogenes, A Sexton of Rome*

Ambrose, *De excessu satyri* and *De officiis ministrorum*
Apostolic Constitutions
Ashby, T., *The Roman Campagna in Classical Times,* 1927
Augustine, *Confessiones* and *Contra Faustum*
Carcopino, J., *Daily Life in Ancient Rome,* 1941
Chrysostom, *De St. Pelagia Virgine et martyres, Homiliae 1* and *In Epistolam ad Hebraeos, Homilia IV*
Clement, *Paedagogus*
Cyprian, *De mortalitate*
Eusebius, *Historia ecclesiastica* and *Vita Constantini*

Fabretti, R., *Inscriptionum antiquarum, quae in paternis aedibus asservantur, explicatio,* 1699

Faustus of Riez, *De septem gradibus ecclesiae*

Geoghegan, A. T., *The Attitude towards Labour in Early Christianity and Ancient Culture,* 1945

Gregory Nazianzus, *Oratio III*

Hilary of Arles, *Sermo de vita St. Honorati*

Jerome, *Vita Pauli; Contra Jovinianum;* and *Epistolae*

Marruchi, O., *Christian Epigraphy,* 1912

Martigny, J. A., *Dictionnaire des antiquités chrétiennes,* 1865

Platner, S. B., and T. Ashby, *A Topographical Dictionary of Ancient Rome,* 1929

Pseudo-Dionysus, *De ecclesiastica hierarchia*

Prudentius, *Cathemerinon* and *Pertistephanon*

Rossi, G. B. de, *Inscriptiones christianae urbis Romae,* 1861

Serapion, *Sacramentary*

Tertullian, *Opera*

Tuker, M. A. R., and Hope Malleson, *Handbook to Christian and Ecclesiastical Rome,* 1900

Vitruvius, *De architectura*

Withrow, W. H., *The Catacombs of Rome,* 1898

5. *John, A Bishop of Constantinople*

Ambrose, *De officiis ministrorum; De virginibus;* and *De virginitate*

Apostolic Constitutions

Augustine, *De virginitate* and *De vita clericorum*

Brightman, F. E., *Liturgies Eastern and Western,* 1896

Chrysostom, *Opera*

Dix, G., *The Shape of the Liturgy,* 1945

Dudden, F. H., *The Life and Times of St. Ambrose,* 1935

Eusebius, *Vita Constantini*

Labarte, J., *Le palais impérial de Constantinople,* 1861

Martroye, F., "*Une sentence arbitrale de Saint-Ambroise*," *Revue Historique de Droit Français et Etranger,* 1929
Millingen, A. Van, *Byzantine Constantinople,* 1899
Palladius, *Dialogus de vita Chrysostomi*
Puech, A., *St. Jean Chrysostome et les moeurs de son temps,* 1891
Schneider, A. F., *Byzanz,* 1936
Singer, C., *A Short History of Medicine,* 1928
Socrates, *Historia ecclesiastica*
Sozomen, *Historia ecclesiastica*

6. *John Cassian, A Monk of Marseilles*

Anan-Isho, *The Book of Paradise,* Syriac text with English translation by E. A. Wallis Budge, 1904
Basil, *Regulae fusius tractatae; Regulae brevius tractatae;* and *Sermo asceticus*
Busquet, R., *Histoire de Marseille,* 1945
Cassian, *Opera*
Chrysostom, *In Matthaeum, Homilia* LV
Jerome, *Regulae Pachomii* and *Epistolae*
Palladius, *Historia Lausiaca*
Sozomen, *Historia ecclesiastica*
Vitae Patrum

APPENDIX II

Books for Further Reading

Although there are no books which are directly concerned with the daily life of the early Christians, there are many which serve to fill out the picture and may be read with pleasure and profit. Foremost among these are contemporary documents, the majority of which are available in translation.

Clement's *Paedagogus,* the most readable of his works and full of interesting information, is translated in the Ante-Nicene Christian Library. E. C. E. Owen, *Some Authentic Acts of the Early Martyrs* (1927), prints twelve accounts from Polycarp in 155 to Procopius in 303; this may be supplemented by A. J. Mason, *The Historic Martyrs of the Primitive Church* (1905), which contains extensive extracts of the early records. Chrysostom's voluminous works were published by Parker of Oxford in the middle of the last century, and the *Conferences* and *Institutes* of Cassian are to be found in the Library of Nicene and Post-Nicene Fathers. Further anecdotes and sayings of the monks appear in E. A. Wallis Budge, *Stories of the Holy Fathers* and *Wit and Wisdom of the Christian Fathers of Egypt* (1935), while Helen Waddell in *The Desert Fathers* (1936), provides translations of many fascinating and amusing accounts.

Besides the original documents themselves, there are several careful studies of the individuals depicted in this present work. R. B. Tollinton's *Clement of Alexandria* (1914), though in two volumes, well deserves attention; H. B. Workman's *Persecution in the Early Church* (1906) is a careful and vivid account; W. R. W. Stephens's *Life of St. Chrysostom* (1880) is not out of date; and much more recently O. Chadwick's *John Cassian* (1950) is certainly to be recommended. There is, as far as I am aware, no study of the work of the sextons, but W. Lowrie, *Christian Art and Archaeology* (1901), though shown by recent research to be inaccurate in his dating, is not incorrect in his description of the catacombs.

Finally, there are works which provide incidental details. J. W. Clark, *The Care of Books* (1901), records the appointments and the development of the early libraries; G. Jennison, *Animals for Show and Pleasure in Ancient Rome* (1937), takes us behind the scenes in the great amphitheaters; G. Dix, *The Shape of the Liturgy* (1945), traces the development of the central act of Christian worship; C. Singer, *A Short History of Medicine* (1928), as its title implies, gives information about the hospitals and methods of healing; and J. G. Davies, *The Origin and Development of Early Christian Architecture* (1952), describes the plans and furniture of the churches during this period.

APPENDIX III

The Nature and Scope of Church Social History

The study of history in the present century has undergone a profound and perceptible change which is both a reaction and a synthesis. It is a reaction to the rationalist school which regarded history as a science, the facts of which could be tabulated and analyzed and their cause and effect discerned independently of the interpretation in which they were first embodied and handed down. The analogy of the physical sciences misled historians as to the truth of their profession, so that they neglected the art of narrative and despised its inseparable companion — imagination. So far from re-creating the past and making it real to those who read it, they mainly exhumed dead bones — the more the better. There can be little doubt that this did much harm to the study of history, cutting off the general reading public from the works of scholarship which were produced with the tenuous and barren brilliance of a factory-made article. Hence the reaction; and so many historians have returned to the view that history is an art and they find their models, not in the rationalism of Seeley, but in the great tradition founded by Clarendon and continued by such men as Gibbon, Carlyle and Macaulay. But the relative value of the scientific method has not been lost in the succeeding synthesis. The study of history today, most would agree, except for those with minds rendered inflexible by a rigid ideology, comprises both scientific, imaginative and literary elements.[1] The scientific element is the accumulation of facts and the sifting of evidence; the imaginative is the selecting and interrelating of these facts, while the literary is the exposition of the results of science and imagination in a form that will arrest and educate the reading public.

This change in the conception of the nature of history has been accompanied by a widening of its content, partly by the correlation of its previous ingredients of past politics and economics.[2] It is now generally recognized that history is concerned not only with great events, with famous statesmen, with battles and victories, with moral lessons and political wisdom, but also with the common daily life of our ancestors, with their work and their play, with their manners and their dress, presented in an imaginative and literary form. Hence the emergence into the whole complex field of historical research of the new subject of study known as social history, whose scope, in the words of Trevelyan, "is the daily life of the inhabitants of the land in past ages: this includes the human as well as the economic relation of different classes to one another, the character of family and household life, the conditions of labour and leisure."[3] Here poetry and truth, reason and imagination are wedded. If one of the elements of historical study is imagination, it is equally true that the appeal of history is imaginative; the imagination longs to see our ancestors

[1] G. M. Trevelyan, *Clio, a Muse, and Other Essays,* 1930, p. 160.

[2] Economic history itself was not established as a study in its own right until some seventy years ago.

[3] *English Social History,* 1945, p. vii.

as they really were, engaged in the manifold activities of day-to-day living. In the pages of social history, at least from the pen of such a literary master as Trevelyan himself, the past is indeed re-created, ceasing to be a memorial of dead people and becoming instead a present living reality.

Ecclesiastical historians have so far been slow to enter into this new field of study. The history of the Church still continues to be a succession of great names and of outstanding events, of popes and schisms, of missionaries and crusades. But this is only, as it were, the "political" history of the Church; its "social" history still remains to be written. There are, however, two qualifications to this sweeping generalization.

In the first place, any and every historical survey of the Church must needs contain some reference to the social environment of its members. No commentary on St. Paul's First Epistle to the Corinthians, for example, could be considered adequate which did not relate it to the social background of which the letter is itself so full. Again, several accounts of the life of the early Church include descriptions of the devotional life of the faithful, of their meeting together for the breaking of bread, of their agapes and of their private prayers;[4] but however accurate such representations may be, Church social history involves more than this; it involves the whole of the Christian's daily life — not only his devotions, both public and private, but his work and his leisure. These descriptions cover part of the ground, but they leave large portions of it unexplored.

The second qualification to the statement that the social

[4] For example, E. von Dobschütz, *Christian Life in the Primitive Church*, E.T., 1904; cf. C. Bigg, *Wayside Sketches in Ecclesiastical History*, 1906, pp. 1–83.

history of the Church still remains to be written is a more important one: that at certain periods it is impossible to distinguish between Church social history and what, for want of a better term may be called "secular" social history. In the Middle Ages the influence of the Church penetrated social relations through and through; the Church was part of the social structure and its organization was inextricably involved in that of the community.[5] The welding together of sacred and secular entirely rules out, in Western Europe at least, any precise distinction between secular and Church social history; to record one is to record the other — for example, Dr. J. H. R. Moorman's *Church Life in England in the Thirteenth Century* (1940) cannot truly be assigned to either separately, for both are fused.[6] Nor in the medieval period is it possible to maintain the distinction on other grounds by saying that the secular social historian will indeed mention the regular round of services and the public religious festivities in which individuals took part, religion remaining for him only one activity among many, while the Church social historian will concentrate upon the spiritual life of the individual, his description of the other aspects of his daily life being conditioned by an attempt to show how that daily life was an expression of his faith and worship. Such a distinction is untenable since any social historian must present not only the small details of life but the attitude of mind of those engaged therein, and in the Middle Ages this attitude was conditioned by the all-pervading authority of

[5] F. M. Powicke, *The Christian Life in the Middle Ages,* 1935, pp. 1–30.

[6] This fusion is nowhere better illustrated than in the pages of John Myrc's *Instructions for Parish Priests* (Early English Text Society, 31, ed. by F. Peacock, 1868).

the Church. Hence all social studies of the medieval period are essentially studies of Church social history — nevertheless, outside these limits the distinction may reasonably be asserted.

In the first three centuries of the Christian era, sacred and secular were clearly distinct.[7] The Christian was in the world but not of it, a sojourner and a pilgrim; to Tertullian he was a "foreigner in this world, a citizen of Jerusalem, the city above." [8] He took no interest in public affairs and one day was the same as another since "he who hopes for eternity from God [does not] calculate the seasons of earth any more." [9] As Israel of old, so the Church remained a people apart, obedient to the government, but hostile to imperial culture and having no real share in the life of secular society. Refusing to serve on the city councils, self-excluded from many trades, restricted in their social intercourse, Christians were indeed a "third race," "creatures of an alien underworld" in Toynbee's phrase, and their social history is almost totally distinct from that of the anti-Christian society in which they had to live. It is true that a limited number of statements by the early patristic writers may be adduced against this assertion; thus Tertullian affirms: "We dwell beside you, sharing your mode of life, dress and habits. We are not Brahmins or Indian gymnosophists dwelling in woods and exiled from life. We live beside you in the world, making use of the same forum, market, bath, shop, inn, and all other places

[7] "Sacred" here is used in reference to Christianity; "sacred" in reference to pagan religion was certainly not distinct from secular in this period, witness the imperial cult among many others.

[8] *De cor.*, xiii.

[9] Cyprian, *De lap.*, ii; hence the late development of the Church's calendar.

of trade."[10] To similar effect the author of the Epistle to Diognetus declares: "Christians are not distinguished from the rest of mankind either in locality or in speech or in customs. For they do not dwell somewhere in cities of their own, neither do they use some different language, nor practice an extraordinary manner of life."[11] But these are the arguments of apologists, anxious to win the good will of their pagan audiences, and if we set beside the quotation of Tertullian his other statement given above, and if we continue the citation of the passage from the Epistle to Diognetus, the essential dichotomy becomes again apparent, and indeed can only be obscured by wrenching passages from their context: "But while Christians dwell in cities of Greeks and barbarians, as the lot of each is cast, and follow the native customs in dress, food and other arrangements of life,[12] yet the constitution of their own citizenship which they set forth is marvelous, and confessedly contradicts expectation. They dwell in their own countries, but only as sojourners."

The conversion of Constantine was destined ultimately to lead to the dissolution of this social dualism, but the way had already been prepared at the beginning of the third century by Origen at Alexandria. Origen was essentially a Hellenist and he broke away from the concrete realism of Christian eschatology which viewed the Kingdom of God as present and the individual Christian as already risen with Christ. For Origen the Kingdom of God is the supersensuous realm of spiritual reality situated in the super-

[10] *Apol.*, xlii.

[11] *Ep. ad Diognetum*, V.

[12] This is indeed special pleading, as the preceding studies will have demonstrated in part.

sensuous and intelligible world; salvation consists in liberation not from the world as such but from the bondage of matter in which the soul is imprisoned. He thus obscured the contrast between the Kingdom of God as a present reality established by Jesus Christ in time and the kingdom of this world as belonging to a past and doomed order, and he was prepared to admit the possibility of a general conversion of the empire. His teaching found its fulfillment in the empire of Constantine which Eusebius, under the influence of Origen, declared to be the Messianic Kingdom, with Constantine as the new David and the Church of the Holy Sepulcher as the New Jerusalem[13] — the kingdom of this world became the Kingdom of God and of His Christ.

Such an attitude was not immediately accepted in the West and the Donatist movement in Africa was in part a protest against any compromise with the world. Augustine himself, while combating the schism, shared their eschatological outlook and expressed it in his doctrine of the two cities, the City of God and the city of man; but by equating the City of God with the realm of transcendent being and the earthly reign of Christ with the Church militant, he lent his support to the Origenist position, for to both "the ideal of the Kingdom of God acquired a metaphysical form, and became identified with the ultimate timeless reality of spiritual being." [14] Augustine, however, differed from Origen in recognizing the importance of the temporal process, of history, which finds its fulfillment in eternity; it was he who both analyzed and defined the significance of events in time, a significance which was implicit in Christianity,

[13] *Vit. Const.*, III, xxxiii.
[14] *A Monument to St. Augustine*, 1930, p. 67.

based as it is on sacred history, but which Augustine was the first to formulate. He thus synthetized the many ideas which impinged upon the Church once it had come to terms with the empire. So by the first quarter of the fifth century the basis of the medieval synthesis had been established, sacred and secular were in process of fusion, and any distinction between Church and secular social history becomes henceforth progressively more and more impossible;[15] before this date, however, the distinction is valid and the sphere of Church social history in the early period is almost uncharted.

In the United States the Catholic University of America has published several books which purport to come within the confines of this subject. In particular there is M. E. Keenan's *The Life and Times of St. Augustine as Revealed in His Letters* (1935), M. M. Fox's *The Life and Times of St. Basil the Great as Revealed in His Works* (1939) and T. A. Goggin's *The Times of Saint Gregory of Nyssa as Reflected in the Letters and the Contra Eunomium* (1947). Unfortunately these studies have adopted what Dr. Farrer terms so accurately "the method of the research-degree thesis";[16] they are little more than painstaking compilations of all the references to so-called social subjects, from anatomy to zoology, arranged under the appropriate headings with necessary grammatical links. The scientific view certainly predominates in the work of these three Roman Catholic nuns, so that their efforts, while valuable to a certain degree, fall short of that imaginative and literary em-

15 This is not to say that in the medieval synthesis there were not present numerous centripetal tendencies, for example, the constant quarrels of pope and emperor and the growth of the eremetical movement whose members inevitably turned their backs on society.

16 A. Farrer, *The Glass of Vision*, 1948, p. 45.

bodiment which would alone entitle them to be classified as Church social history. Hence the generalization that Church social history[17] remains to be written may be accepted as true within the limits defined, the generalization being qualified by the recognition that this does not apply to the medieval period.

The purpose of medieval culture was to establish the City of God upon earth,[18] to this end it subordinated everything, and its emphasis upon asceticism and devotion, upon spiritual authority and discipline, led eventually to a restriction of the free play of man's creative energies. It was a glorious failure, and it failed because it concentrated those same energies upon interior spiritual matters without giving them adequate expression in exterior forms. The Renaissance and the Reformation were in part a revolt against this constriction, and modern history which begins with these movements is the attempt "to discover man's potentialities" [19] in the sphere of nature as well as in that of religion. Both the Renaissance and the Reformation involved the repudiation of the supreme authority of the Church, which had been the linchpin of the medieval synthesis;[20] with the dissolution of this synthesis, the one movement emphasized the classical elements, thus rediscovering the antique, while the other sought to free the Biblical doctrines from these elements. Thus sacred and

[17] It should be noted that, to employ Butterfield's terminology, this is "technical" history and not "general" history. (H. Butterfield, *Christianity and History,* 1950, pp. 17–25.)

[18] Augustine himself, however, never identified the *Civitas Dei* with any earthly state; cf. J. N. Figgis, *The Political Aspects of St. Augustine's "City of God,"* 1921.

[19] N. Berdyaev, *The Meaning of History,* 1945, p. 20.

[20] R. E. Davies, *The Problem of Authority in the Continental Reformers,* 1946.

secular once more began to disjoin, until in the present century in the West they are almost entirely separate again.[21] Hence Church social history, the record of the Christian's daily life springing from his religious beliefs, becomes once again a branch of study distinct from secular social history, the record of daily life in which religion is only one element and regrettably one of the least important elements.

There are two principal methods of presenting social history. The first, adopted by Trevelyan himself, may be termed the generalized descriptive method, that is, the imaginative representation of the facts without emphasis upon any particular individual — the portrayal of a class or classes, of a guild or a profession, the outlining of "a series of scenes divided by intervals of time."[22] The alternative, which is not open to the charge of vagueness (because of its lack of outstanding personalities) often brought against the first, is the method followed by the late Dr. Eileen Power in her *Medieval People* (1924), in which she personified the general facts of medieval social history, depicting them in the composite portraits of specific individuals, whether peasant life in the character of Bodo, whose name appears in the estate book of a manorial lord, or monastic life in the person of Madame Eglentyne, who, although a fictitious creation of Chaucer, nevertheless, is typical of the religious life she professed. It is this second method which has been adopted in the present work, but to employ the method of personification is to place oneself in a posi-

[21] It is interesting to remark that this swing of the pendulum is accompanied in the twentieth century by a renewed persecution of the Church and by a revived appreciation of eschatology which can only be compared with that of the early Christian period.

[22] *English Social History*, p. 11.

tion of initial disadvantage as compared with him who chooses the generalized descriptive method. The latter can use a large canvas, painting his picture with broad bold sweeps; the former, to continue the metaphor, is painting a miniature which will be ineffective if many details are omitted and therefore he is the more subservient to his sources. When the details cannot be discovered he must either relinquish his method or pass on to another period for which sufficient precise information is available. Thus, for example, he may wish to describe the daily life of a presbyter in the pre-Nicene period, but that is impossible; a general account may be given, but even the incisive treatises of Tertullian, the vigorous descriptions of Clement, the remains of the prolific Origen and the carefully phrased letters of Cyprian provide few hints to enable one to follow a third-century parish priest through his day hour by hour. This dependence upon detailed sources explains, more than anything else, the selection of subjects in this study, although the attempt has been made to present as varied and representative an account as the written and archaeological evidence allows in the choice of vocation and geographical setting, as well as in date. It was, of course, tempting to record some of the more unusual features of early Church life, to describe the thoughts and practices of a St. Simeon Stylites who for thirty-six years lived on the top of a stone pillar, or of the Alexandrian maidservant who spent ten years in a tomb, or of the monk who retired to a tub suspended in mid-air; but interesting and diverting though these people were, and despite their many imitators, they cannot be deemed representative of Christian life as a whole in the first five centuries.

Index

Index